GATLINBURG TRAVEL GUIDE 2025

Explore the Best Attractions, Outdoor Adventures, and Hidden Gems in the Heart of the Smoky Mountains

Albert N. Allred

Disclaimer

"We've put great effort into creating the Gatlinburg Travel Guide 2025 to provide you with the most accurate and comprehensive information available for this wonderful destination. However, details like prices, operating hours, and tour schedules may be subject to change. For the smoothest possible experience, we advise that you double-check these details directly with the respective hotels, accommodations, and attractions before starting your Gatlinburg journey. While this guide is intended as a helpful tool for planning your trip, taking a moment to verify this information will ensure your time in Gatlinburg is as enjoyable and memorable as possible."

Table of Contents

GATLINBURG MAP

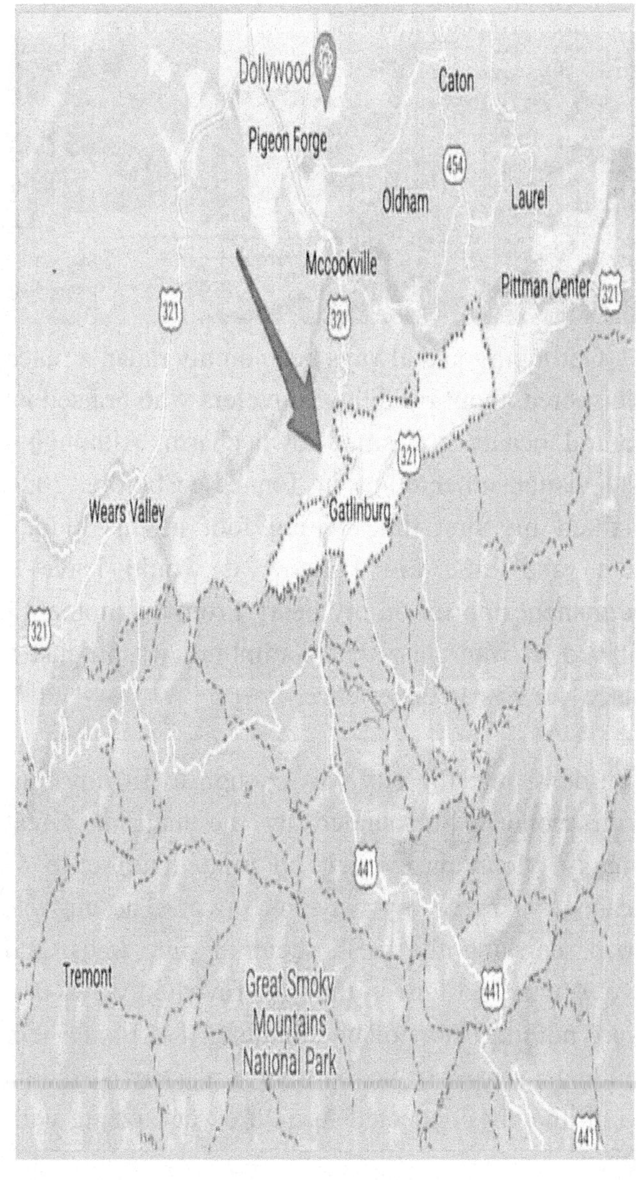

Introduction

Gatlinburg had always been on my radar, a place whispered about by fellow travelers who praised its natural beauty and small-town charm. Although I had visited other cities in Tennessee before, 2024 marked my first time setting foot in this hidden gem, and little did I know it would leave a permanent imprint on my heart. From the moment I arrived, it was clear that Gatlinburg wasn't just a place—it was an experience.

The drive into the city was enough to fill my soul with wonder. Surrounded by the majestic Great Smoky Mountains, I felt an immediate sense of peace as I made my way into town. The air was crisp, carrying the fresh scent of pine trees, and every twist and turn in the road revealed views that were nothing short of breathtaking. I couldn't help but feel a sense of awe that such a place existed, one so intimately connected to nature yet buzzing with life.

My first day began with a visit to the Great Smoky Mountains National Park. Hiking had always been one of my favourite ways to explore, and this was no exception. The trail I chose led me through towering trees and across babbling brooks, and it wasn't long before I reached a stunning waterfall hidden deep within the forest. The sight of it, cascading down rocks worn smooth by time, took my breath away. I remember standing there, feeling completely at one with the world, as the sound of rushing water and birdsong filled the air. It was in that moment that Gatlinburg captured a part of me I didn't know could be reached.

One of the most memorable experiences was taking the Gatlinburg SkyLift. As the chairlift carried me high above the treetops, I saw the town below like a little cluster of stories waiting to be told, while the mountains stretched endlessly beyond. The view from the top was surreal—rolling hills painted in every shade of green, fading into the horizon as the sun began its slow descent. I remember feeling a quiet sense of joy, knowing I was part of something much bigger than myself.

As night fell, Gatlinburg transformed into something almost magical. The streets, lit with the warm glow of lanterns, were filled with the sounds of laughter and the smell of delicious Southern food. I found myself wandering through the charming shops, each offering unique handmade crafts and souvenirs that seemed to tell the story of the town itself. My evening ended with a hearty meal in one of the cosy local restaurants, where I was treated to authentic Southern cooking that warmed my heart just as much as it filled my belly.

My time in Gatlinburg was short, but it was rich with memories. This mountain town, with its blend of natural beauty and welcoming spirit, had given me an experience I would never forget. As I packed my bags to leave, I couldn't shake the feeling that this wasn't a goodbye, but rather the beginning of a new love for a place I would return to again and again. Gatlinburg, with all its wonder, had won me over completely.

BEST RIBS
CALHOUN'S
IN AMERICA
SPREAD SOME HOLIDAY
CHEER BUY YOUR

Chapter 1: Discovering Gatlinburg

A. A Brief History of Gatlinburg

Gatlinburg is a town that has grown through history, shaped by the resilience of its people and its connection to the Great Smoky Mountains. Originally called White Oak Flats due to the abundance of native white oak trees, the area was first settled in the early 1800s by William Ogle and his family. William Ogle, who found what he called the "Land of Paradise" in these Appalachian Mountains, started building a cabin but tragically died of malaria before he could bring his family. In 1807, his widow Martha Jane Huskey Ogle and their children moved to complete his dream, settling in what is now Gatlinburg. Their cabin still stands today, serving as a significant historical landmark that you can visit in downtown Gatlinburg, giving you a tangible glimpse into the area's pioneering days.

Gatlinburg's name came from a rather colorful character named Radford Gatlin. Arriving around 1854, Gatlin opened the town's second general store and established a post office in his shop, which led to the area being named after him. Though Gatlin was known for his flamboyant and controversial personality, and eventually clashed with many in the community, his name stuck. Interestingly, even after he was forced to leave due to disputes with other settlers, the town continued to bear his name, a legacy that continues to this day.

In the years following the Civil War, Gatlinburg remained a modest mountain settlement. However, the 20th century brought significant changes, especially with the establishment of the Great Smoky Mountains National Park in 1934. The creation of the park, which today is the most visited in the United States, transformed Gatlinburg from a small town dependent on farming and logging into a major tourist gateway. The national park not only preserved the stunning landscapes but also brought economic prosperity through tourism, setting Gatlinburg on a path of steady growth and popularity.

The early 1900s also saw the influence of organizations like the Pi Beta Phi women's fraternity, which established the Arrowmont School of Arts and Crafts. This initiative aimed to bring education and opportunities to the community, and today, Arrowmont remains a hub of creativity, preserving and promoting the crafts that are an essential part of the Appalachian heritage.

Gatlinburg's charm lies in its ability to balance its historic roots with modern tourism. Walking through its streets today, you can explore sites like the Historic Ogle Cabin, visit the Great Smoky Arts and Crafts Community, and see how this little settlement evolved into the bustling tourist hub it is today. Moreover, sustainability is a big part of the town's ethos now. Gatlinburg has embraced sustainable tourism, ensuring that the natural beauty of the Smokies is preserved for future generations. Initiatives like "Leave No Trace" encourage responsible travel, and there are many local programs working towards the conservation of the region’s unique ecosystem.

B. Best Time to Visit

Spring (March to May) is an excellent time for those who enjoy milder weather and blooming nature. As spring sets in, the Great Smoky Mountains come to life with wildflowers in vibrant colours. During this season, the mountains are known for their "Spring Wildflower Pilgrimage," an event where you can see hundreds of varieties of wildflowers as well as guided hikes and educational programs. Temperatures typically range from 10°C to 20°C (50°F to 70°F), making it ideal for outdoor activities like hiking, biking, or visiting local attractions. With smaller crowds compared to summer, you can enjoy Gatlinburg at a more relaxed pace while soaking in its natural beauty.

Summer (June to August) is peak season for Gatlinburg, filled with activities for families and adventure seekers. This is the time of year when the town is bustling with visitors enjoying everything from mountain coasters to river tubing. Kids are out of school, and families take the opportunity to visit attractions like Ripley's Aquarium of the Smokies and Ober Gatlinburg. If you love being active outdoors, this is the time for whitewater rafting, zip-lining, and exploring the many trails. The summer temperatures are warm, generally ranging from 25°C to 30°C (77°F to 86°F), making the cool mountain breezes even more welcoming. Be prepared for crowds, as summer is one of the busiest times in Gatlinburg, but this also means the town is in full swing with a lot of energy and activities.

Fall (September to November) is arguably the most scenic time to visit Gatlinburg. As autumn arrives, the lush greenery of the Smokies begins to transform into stunning shades of orange, red, and gold. The famous fall foliage draws in tourists, making this one of the most popular times to visit. You can experience this splendour through scenic drives, hikes, or even a ride on the Gatlinburg SkyLift, which provides a panoramic view of the autumn colours. Temperatures during the day can range from 15°C to 25°C (59°F to 77°F), making it comfortable for exploration. October, in particular, is known for its fall festivals and the Smoky Mountain Harvest Festival, where local artisans and vendors showcase crafts and goods, giving you a taste of Appalachian culture.

Winter (December to February) transforms Gatlinburg into a winter wonderland. With festive lights decorating the streets and a blanket of snow occasionally covering the mountains, it's a magical time to visit. Winter is perfect for visitors who want to ski or snowboard, as Ober Gatlinburg offers both winter sports and family fun. The temperatures can get quite cold, ranging between -6°C to 10°C (20°F to 50°F), but the festive atmosphere of the holidays makes it a special experience. The annual Gatlinburg Winter Magic event runs from November through February, featuring millions of LED lights that illuminate the town, making evening strolls especially delightful. It's also a quieter time compared to summer, which might appeal to those who prefer fewer crowds.

Each season has its unique attractions, making Gatlinburg a year-round destination. If you're looking for fewer crowds and a more relaxed experience, spring and winter are ideal times to plan your trip. On the other hand, if you enjoy festivals, lively streets, and family fun, then summer or fall will offer just what you're looking for. No matter when you decide to visit, the town's charm and the surrounding Smoky Mountains promise an unforgettable experience.

In the end, the best time to visit depends on what you want to experience—whether it's the floral blooms of spring, the vibrant buzz of summer activities, the enchanting autumn foliage, or the peaceful winter landscapes. Gatlinburg has something for everyone, year-round, ensuring that every visit has its own magic.

C. Why Gatlinburg is a Must-See Destination in 2025

Natural Beauty and Gateway to the Smokies
Gatlinburg's biggest draw is its proximity to the Great Smoky Mountains National Park, the most visited national park in the United States. In 2025, the park is offering new and improved experiences

for visitors, such as expanded guided tours and upgraded amenities, which means your journey through nature is going to be even more memorable. Imagine hiking to see cascading waterfalls, breathing in the crisp mountain air, or just relaxing by a quiet stream while surrounded by majestic peaks. And with the park's new conservation efforts, you can be sure your visit is both enjoyable and environmentally friendly.

Whether it's hiking in the warmer months or seeing the scenic snow-covered peaks in winter, the park is always a highlight of visiting Gatlinburg. In 2025, more trails are accessible with enhanced signage and guided programs that aim to bring people closer to nature while preserving its beauty. Plus, there are more eco-friendly tours available, allowing you to explore without a large environmental footprint.

Unique Attractions and Activities

Gatlinburg has so many attractions that you'll never run out of things to do. The town offers everything from family-friendly spots like Ripley's Aquarium of the Smokies to thrilling adventures like Anakeesta, a mountaintop park that now features expanded zip-lining and a newly opened tree canopy walk. In 2025, Ober Gatlinburg, the popular amusement park and ski area, has also introduced more family-centric activities, including new roller coasters and educational wildlife exhibits. This combination of entertainment options makes Gatlinburg a versatile vacation spot for people of all ages.

The Gatlinburg Space Needle is another favourite. This iconic attraction has updated its viewing experience with augmented reality binoculars in 2025, giving you a more immersive look at the Smokies and the vibrant town below. Not to mention the bustling downtown filled with charming shops, restaurants serving up Southern delicacies, and unique attractions that make every moment fun-filled and special.

Appalachian Culture and Heritage

For those interested in culture, Gatlinburg is a treasure trove of Appalachian history and traditions. In 2025, the town continues to promote its arts and crafts heritage with the Gatlinburg Arts and Crafts Community, the largest group of independent artisans in North America. Here, you can find handmade pottery, paintings, and woven goods that reflect the Appalachian way of life. These artisans keep the local culture alive, offering workshops that let you take part in the creative process, making your visit more meaningful.

The town's festivals are another reason to visit. Gatlinburg hosts a variety of events throughout the year, such as the Smoky Mountain Tunes & Tales festival, which brings history to life with storytellers, musicians, and craftsmen showcasing the traditions of the region. In 2025, new cultural initiatives have also been introduced, including more interactive events for visitors to connect deeply with the heritage of the Smokies, from traditional bluegrass music sessions to demonstrations of local craft skills.

Sustainable Tourism Efforts

Gatlinburg has embraced sustainable tourism as a key focus for 2025. There are numerous ongoing projects to reduce environmental impact, particularly as it continues to attract more visitors each year. You'll notice many places encourage the "Leave No Trace" principles to protect the natural surroundings. Local businesses are participating in green initiatives, such as sourcing products locally to reduce the carbon footprint and even offering discounts to patrons who choose environmentally conscious options. If you care about responsible travel, Gatlinburg will resonate with your values, giving you a holiday that's both enjoyable and aligned with environmental preservation.

Perfect for All Types of Travellers

Another reason Gatlinburg is a must-see in 2025 is its appeal to various types of travellers. Families will find plenty of activities suitable for children, from the thrilling Ober Gatlinburg adventure park to the fascinating exhibits at Ripley's Aquarium. Couples will love the romantic backdrops provided by the Smoky Mountains, with many places to explore or simply relax and enjoy a cosy getaway. For solo adventurers, Gatlinburg offers plenty of opportunities to meet other travellers, take on the challenges of the numerous trails, or simply lose yourself in the beauty of nature.

Chapter 2: Getting to Gatlinburg

A. Transportation Options to Gatlinburg (Flights, Driving Routes, and Public Transport)

Nearby Airports and How to Get There

If you're planning your journey to Gatlinburg and wondering about the nearest airports and how best to travel from them, don't worry—there are a few excellent options to help you get here comfortably. Whether you prefer convenience or scenery, there's an airport and route perfect for you.

1. McGhee Tyson Airport (TYS)

McGhee Tyson Airport in Knoxville, Tennessee, is the closest major airport to Gatlinburg, situated just about 40 miles away. It's a small but well-equipped airport that offers services from major airlines such as Delta, American Airlines, United Airlines, Allegiant, and Frontier. Known for its friendly service and easy-to-navigate layout, McGhee Tyson Airport serves as a great gateway for those wanting to reach the Smokies with minimal travel hassle. The airport's history dates back to the 1930s, and it has been continuously upgraded to provide modern amenities and efficient services.

From McGhee Tyson Airport, you have multiple options to get to Gatlinburg:

- **Rental Cars:** Available from agencies like Hertz, Avis, Budget, and Enterprise, starting from about $45-$70 per day. Renting a car gives you the flexibility to explore the scenic routes to Gatlinburg.
- **Shuttle Services:** Several shuttle services offer direct transfers from the airport to Gatlinburg, with prices ranging from $60-$100 per person. These shuttles provide a comfortable and convenient option for those who would rather not drive themselves.
- **Rideshares and Taxis:** You can also opt for rideshare services like Uber and Lyft, though availability may vary, and the cost is around $70-$90 for the one-hour ride.

You can find more information or book services on their website: [FlyKnoxville.com](https://flyknoxville.com)

2. Asheville Regional Airport (AVL)

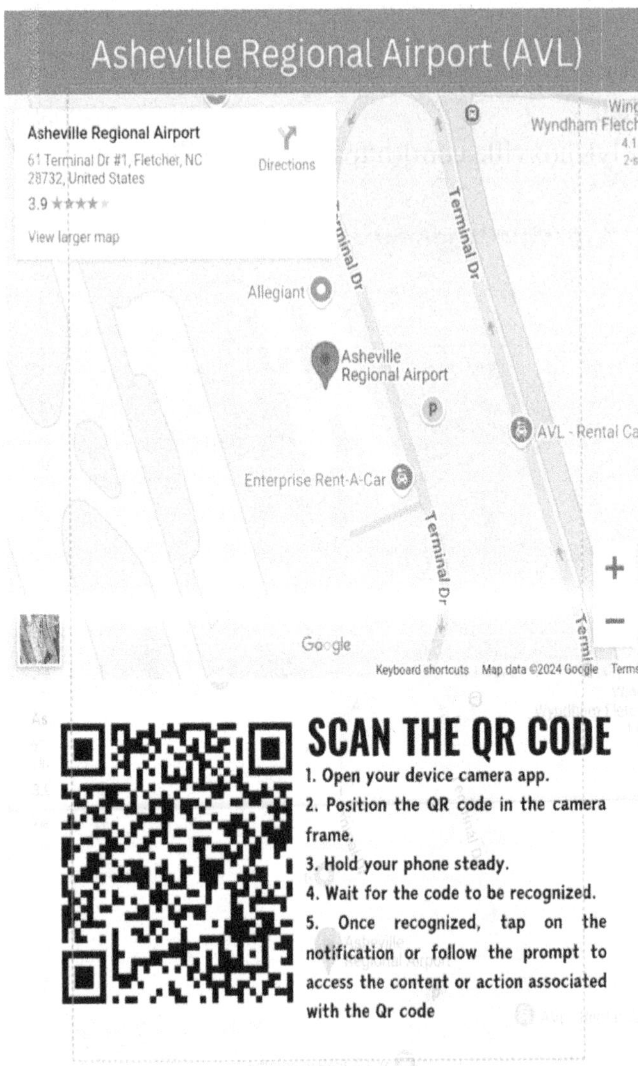

SCAN THE QR CODE

1. Open your device camera app.
2. Position the QR code in the camera frame.
3. Hold your phone steady.
4. Wait for the code to be recognized.
5. Once recognized, tap on the notification or follow the prompt to access the content or action associated with the Qr code

Located about 90 miles from Gatlinburg, Asheville Regional Airport is another viable option, especially if you’d like to explore the North Carolina side of the Smokies. The airport, established in 1961, is served by major carriers like American Airlines, Delta, United, and JetBlue, offering a good selection of flights from various locations across the country.

Getting to Gatlinburg from Asheville is a pleasant drive through the mountains, taking around two hours, but the views make every mile worth it. Here’s how you can get to Gatlinburg from Asheville:

- **Rental Cars:** Available from the airport, with costs starting at around $45 per day, renting a car is recommended, especially if you wish to make the most of the scenic route through the Smokies.
- **Shuttle Services:** Shuttle services from Asheville Regional Airport to Gatlinburg are available, with costs ranging between $80-$120, depending on the service provider and your travel dates.
- **Taxis and Rideshares:** While not as common, you can find taxis or book rides through Uber and Lyft, though it's always advisable to check availability ahead of time.

You can learn more and book your transportation on their website: [FlyAVL.com](https://flyavl.com).

3. Charlotte Douglas International Airport (CLT)

If you're flying in from a farther destination or prefer more flight options, Charlotte Douglas International Airport is an excellent choice, located approximately 190 miles away. Charlotte Douglas is one of the largest and busiest airports in the southeastern United States, handling both domestic and international flights. Established in 1935, the airport has grown to become a major hub, with excellent facilities and services.

Here's how to make your way to Gatlinburg from Charlotte:

- **Car Rentals:** Car rentals are available from a range of providers at Charlotte Douglas, and this is probably the best option if you don't mind a road trip. The drive takes roughly four hours, with rental costs starting at around $50 per day.
- **Shuttle Services:** Shuttles from Charlotte to Gatlinburg can be arranged, but given the distance, this can be quite pricey—often ranging from $150-$200 per person. It may be worth it if you're travelling in a group or looking for comfort.

For flight bookings and further details, check the official website: [CLT Airport's official website](https://cltairport.com).

4. Tri-Cities Airport (TRI)

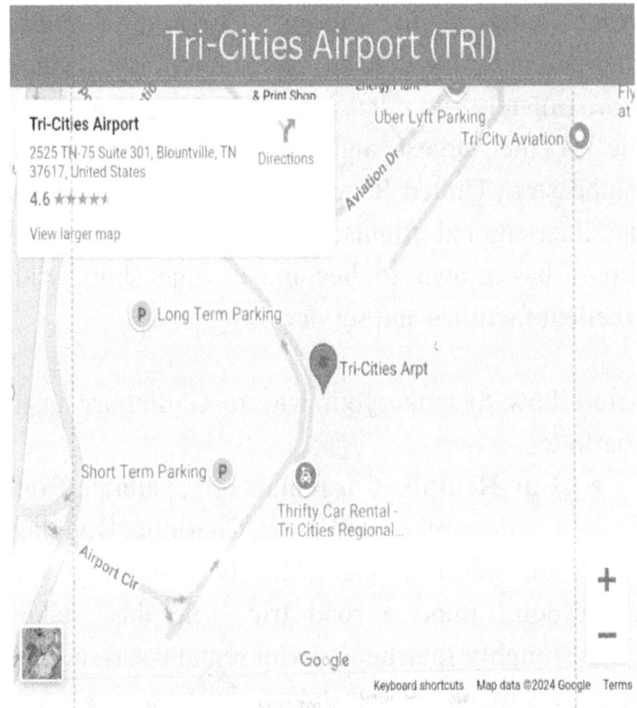

SCAN THE QR CODE

1. Open your device camera app.
2. Position the QR code in the camera frame.
3. Hold your phone steady.
4. Wait for the code to be recognized.
5. Once recognized, tap on the notification or follow the prompt to access the content or action associated with the Qr code

Tri-Cities Airport is located in Blountville, Tennessee, about 100 miles northeast of Gatlinburg. It's a small regional airport that serves airlines like Allegiant, Delta, and American, providing connections from several major cities. If you're looking for an alternative to the bigger airports, this is a good option.

- **Rental Cars:** Available on-site, with average daily rates starting at $45.
- **Taxis and Shuttles:** While taxis are available, shuttle services are recommended for a more comfortable journey to Gatlinburg.

More information can be found on their website: [Tri-Cities Airport](https://triflight.com).

Getting to Gatlinburg from the Airports

From each of these airports, driving is typically the most convenient way to get to Gatlinburg. If you choose to rent a car, you'll find that the routes are well-signposted and easy to navigate. The journey from Knoxville's McGhee Tyson Airport takes about 1-1.5 hours via US-129 North and US-441 South, offering scenic views as you approach the Smokies.

From Asheville Regional Airport, the route involves taking I-40 West and then joining US-441 North into Gatlinburg, giving you plenty of opportunities to admire the mountain views along the way. The journey is roughly two hours but filled with the charm of the mountains.

From Charlotte Douglas International Airport, take I-85 South and then I-26 West, eventually connecting with US-441. It's a longer drive, but if you're a road trip enthusiast, the four-hour journey through the foothills of Appalachia will be worth every minute.

For those who prefer not to drive, Gatlinburg's Trolley System offers a free, convenient way to get around the town once you arrive. The trolley system covers all major areas and attractions and runs every day, with no fares required. The main transit center is at Ripley's Aquarium of the Smokies, making it accessible to all visitors. For more information on schedules and routes, you can visit their website: [Gatlinburg Trolley](https://www.gatlinburg.com/trolley) or call (865) 436-3897.

Car Rentals and Local Transport Tips

Once you've landed at one of the nearby airports or driven into the scenic Smoky Mountains, getting around Gatlinburg becomes the next part of the adventure. This section will guide you through everything you need to know about car rentals and getting around locally. Whether you want the flexibility of a rental car or prefer to experience the town on foot or by trolley, Gatlinburg has convenient options for every traveler.

Car Rentals

For those flying in, renting a car is one of the best options to reach Gatlinburg and explore the surrounding areas at your own pace. Each of the nearby airports—McGhee Tyson Airport (TYS) in Knoxville, Asheville Regional Airport (AVL), and Charlotte Douglas International Airport (CLT)—offers a range of car rental services. Here's what you need to know:

- **McGhee Tyson Airport (Knoxville, TN):** Car rental agencies such as Hertz, Avis, Enterprise, and Budget operate at McGhee Tyson. Renting a car will give you freedom during your stay, and daily rental costs start at around $45-$70, depending on the car model and rental company. Reservations are recommended, especially during peak travel seasons like summer and fall. You can book online through the airport's official site: [FlyKnoxville.com](https://flyknoxville.com).

- **Asheville Regional Airport (Asheville, NC):** Asheville Regional Airport also offers major car rental services, and since this airport is about a two-hour drive from Gatlinburg, renting a car makes the journey more comfortable and allows you to enjoy the sights at your own pace. Daily rental rates here typically range from $45-$65. Booking ahead of time is encouraged, and more details are available at [FlyAVL.com](https://flyavl.com).

- **Charlotte Douglas International Airport (Charlotte, NC):** For those flying in from a long distance, Charlotte Douglas offers a broader selection of car rental agencies due to its status as a major international airport. Companies like Alamo, National, and Thrifty are available here, with rental prices starting around $50-$80 per day. More information and booking options can be found at [CLT Airport's official website](https://cltairport.com).

B. Local Transport in Gatlinburg

Once you've reached Gatlinburg, you may find that you don't need your rental car as much as expected, especially if you plan to spend most of your time exploring the town. Gatlinburg's compact layout and efficient public transport options make getting around easy and enjoyable.

The Gatlinburg Trolley

The Gatlinburg Trolley is one of the most convenient ways to navigate around town. The trolley is not only iconic but also free to use, operating year-round. There are several routes covering different parts of the town, including popular areas like Downtown Gatlinburg, Great Smoky Arts & Crafts Community, and Ober Gatlinburg. With over 20 trolleys on the road, you can be sure of timely and frequent service to most of Gatlinburg's must-see spots.

The trolleys run out of the Mass Transit Center, which is centrally located at Ripley's Aquarium of the Smokies. Depending on the time of year, the trolley hours vary:

- **March - April:** 10:30 a.m. - 10:00 p.m.
- **May - October:** 8:30 a.m. - Midnight
- **November - February:** Sunday-Thursday 10:30 a.m. - 6:00 p.m.; Fridays and Saturdays until 10:00 p.m.

The convenience of the trolley is further enhanced by Park-n-Ride facilities located at 1011 Banner Road, near the Gatlinburg Welcome Center, allowing you to park your car and catch the trolley into downtown. This saves the hassle of finding parking, especially during busy seasons. You can find more information and download the route map at: [Gatlinburg Trolley](https://www.gatlinburg.com/trolley) or contact them at (865) 436-3897.

Walking and Biking

Walking is one of the best ways to experience Gatlinburg's charm up close. Downtown Gatlinburg is pedestrian-friendly, with sidewalks lining all major streets and crosswalks that make navigating easy. With so many restaurants, shops, and attractions clustered together, exploring on foot often means you can find unexpected gems and enjoy the lively atmosphere of this mountain town.

Walking also allows you to take in the scenery, hear local musicians, and interact with friendly locals at a relaxed pace.

For those who love being active, biking is another option. You can even bike into the Great Smoky Mountains National Park using the Gatlinburg Trail, which is one of only two trails in the park that allow bicycles. This trail runs from Sugarlands Visitor Center into the town, offering a perfect mix of exercise and nature for a day trip.

Ride Share and Taxis

Uber and Lyft are both available in Gatlinburg and provide another convenient option for getting around, especially if you want to get somewhere quickly or if you're staying outside the main downtown area. A short ride across town will generally cost between $10-$15, while rides to nearby areas like Pigeon Forge are slightly more. Local taxi services also operate in Gatlinburg, providing dependable transport options, especially for those wanting late-night rides or for specific excursions.

Practical Tips for Local Transport

- **Parking in Gatlinburg:** Parking downtown can be a challenge during peak seasons, but there are several public and private lots that charge about $10-$20 per day. Make sure to arrive early to secure a spot, particularly during weekends or holidays.
- **Trolley Schedule:** Plan your day based on the trolley schedule. During the busy summer and fall seasons, the trolleys run late, making it easy to enjoy dinner and shopping without worrying about transport.
- **Consider a Rental Car for Day Trips:** If you're planning to explore Cades Cove, Clingmans Dome, or nearby towns, having a car is a big plus, as these locations aren't served by public transport.

Walgreens
F MARKET
CASTRO
1050

Chapter3: Where to Stay in Gatlinburg

A. Best Hotels and Lodges

1. The Park Vista – A DoubleTree by Hilton Hotel

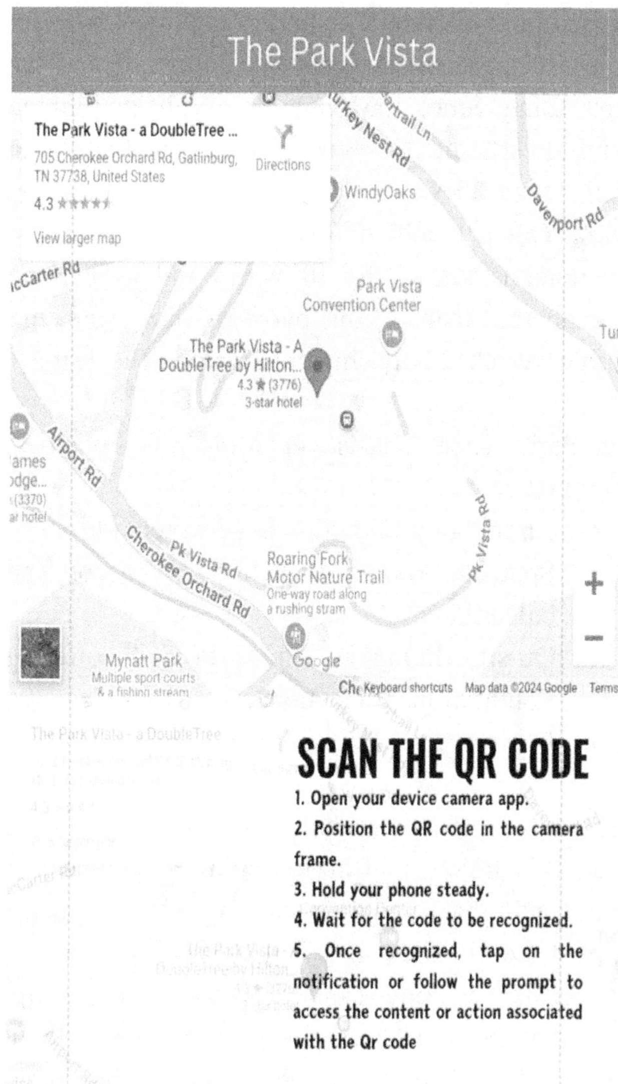

SCAN THE QR CODE

1. Open your device camera app.
2. Position the QR code in the camera frame.
3. Hold your phone steady.
4. Wait for the code to be recognized.
5. Once recognized, tap on the notification or follow the prompt to access the content or action associated with the Qr code

Perched on a hillside, The Park Vista offers some of the most spectacular views of Gatlinburg and the surrounding Smoky Mountains. With its unique round tower structure, every room at The Park Vista offers scenic views, making it perfect for travellers looking for a blend of luxury and natural beauty. The hotel is known for its warm and welcoming atmosphere, thanks in part to the signature DoubleTree chocolate chip cookie upon check-in.

The Park Vista boasts an array of amenities, including:

- An indoor pool with a large waterslide
- Spacious rooms with modern décor and balconies
- On-site dining at The Vista Grill, offering Southern-inspired cuisine
- Fire pits for a cosy evening

With rooms typically starting from $150 to $250 per night, this hotel is ideal for families, couples, or anyone looking to enjoy a comfortable stay in the heart of the Smokies. The Park Vista is located just a short trolley ride from downtown Gatlinburg, making it easy to access local attractions without the hassle of parking. You can find more information or book your stay on their website: [The Park Vista by

Hilton](https://www.hilton.com/en/hotels/gtlpsdt-the-park-vista/).

2. Bearskin Lodge on the River

Bearskin Lodge on the River

Bearskin Lodge
840 River Rd, Gatlinburg, TN 37738, United States
4.5
View larger map
Directions

Car parking
Ober Mountain Tramway Mall
Shopping Centre
River Rd
3.7 (817)
3-star hotel
Bearskin Lodge On the River
4.5 (1091)
3-star hotel
Crockett's Breakfast Camp
Breakfast · $$
Ski Mountain Rd
The Park Grill
American · $$
Motel 6 Gatlinburg, TN - Smoky Mountains
3.1 (1965)
2-star hotel
Parkway
Gatlinburg Trail Trail
Forested area for hiking & biking
Keyboard shortcuts Map data ©2024 Google Terms

SCAN THE QR CODE

1. Open your device camera app.
2. Position the QR code in the camera frame.
3. Hold your phone steady.
4. Wait for the code to be recognized.
5. Once recognized, tap on the notification or follow the prompt to access the content or action associated with the Qr code

For those who want to stay close to nature while still having easy access to the town, Bearskin Lodge on the River is an excellent choice. Located at the edge of the Great Smoky Mountains National Park, Bearskin Lodge offers a rustic yet comfortable atmosphere, with cabin-inspired decor and modern amenities.

Key features include:

- A beautiful riverside location, with some rooms offering balconies overlooking the stream
- A seasonal outdoor pool and lazy river
- Complimentary breakfast and access to nearby hiking trails

Rates at Bearskin Lodge start from $180 per night, and it is popular for its proximity to some of Gatlinburg's best trails and natural attractions. If you're a fan of the outdoors, this lodge is a perfect fit for a quiet yet conveniently located retreat. Visit [Bearskin Lodge Gatlinburg](https://bearskinlodge.com) for booking details.

3. Margaritaville Resort Gatlinburg

For those seeking a relaxed, tropical vibe in the middle of the Smokies, Margaritaville Resort provides a unique and refreshing getaway. Located downtown, this resort offers guests easy access to restaurants, shopping, and attractions, while also providing an oasis of fun and relaxation.

Highlights of Margaritaville Resort include:

- Spacious rooms and suites designed for relaxation, with colorful island-inspired decor
- An outdoor pool with a hot tub and fire pits
- St. Somewhere Spa, where guests can enjoy massages and other treatments
- On-site dining at LandShark Bar & Grill

Rates typically range from $220 to $350 per night, making it a slightly more luxurious option. However, with its array of amenities and easy downtown access, it's a favorite for those looking for a lively yet comfortable stay. For more information, visit [Margaritaville Gatlinburg](https://www.margaritavilleresorts.com/margaritaville-resort-gatlinburg).

4. Greystone Lodge on the River

Greystone Lodge offers comfort, scenic river views, and easy access to Gatlinburg's attractions. The lodge is located right on the Little Pigeon River, providing guests with a peaceful environment while still being close to downtown. The rooms are spacious and feature modern furnishings, with some having private balconies overlooking the river.

The lodge's features include:

- A complimentary breakfast to start your day
- An outdoor pool for warmer months
- Rooms equipped with kitchenettes for convenience

With rates starting at $150 to $220 per night, Greystone Lodge is a great choice for travelers wanting the convenience of downtown Gatlinburg while enjoying a scenic riverfront setting. Bookings can be made through [Greystone Lodge](https://greystonelodgetn.com).

5. Old Creek Lodge

If you want the charm of a rustic mountain cabin but with the amenities of a modern hotel, Old Creek Lodge is the perfect blend. Located within walking distance of attractions like the Gatlinburg SkyBridge and Ripley's Aquarium, Old Creek Lodge provides a cozy retreat after a day of exploration.

Key amenities include:

- Rooms featuring gas fireplaces and private balconies overlooking the creek
- Complimentary breakfast served every morning
- Easy access to both the downtown area and the Great Smoky Mountains National Park

Rates start from $160 per night, making Old Creek Lodge an affordable option for a uniquely Gatlinburg experience. It's a great choice for those who want to be close to everything while still enjoying the sound of a running creek right outside their balcony. More information can be found at [Old Creek Lodge Gatlinburg](https://www.oldcreeklodgegatlinburg.com).

B. Budget-Friendly Accommodations

1. Quality Inn Creekside - Downtown Gatlinburg

For travelers looking for a central location without spending a fortune, Quality Inn Creekside is a perfect choice. Situated right in the heart of Gatlinburg, this hotel offers easy access to major attractions like Ripley's Aquarium of the Smokies and Ober Gatlinburg.

Key Features:

- **Rates:** Starting from $70 per night, Quality Inn Creekside offers great value for money.
- **Location:** It's within walking distance of popular attractions, making it convenient for those who prefer to explore on foot.
- **Amenities:** Rooms are clean and well-equipped, and guests can enjoy complimentary breakfast each morning to start the day right. The hotel also has a seasonal outdoor pool and balconies in some rooms with lovely views of the creek.

For more information or to book, visit [Quality Inn Creekside Gatlinburg](https://www.choicehotels.com/quality-inn).

2. Gatlinburg Town Square by Exploria Resorts

Gatlinburg Town Square by Exploria

Gatlinburg Town Square
515 Airport Rd, Gatlinburg, TN 37738, United States
4.1 ★★★★
View larger map
Directions

Log Cabin Pancake House
Trentham Ln
The Grand Orchard Lodge
Belle Aire Ln
4.4 ★ (2480)
3-star hotel
Popular Ln
Gatlinburg Town Square
4.1 ★ (1536)
3-star hotel
Trinity Ln
Reagan Dr
McCarter Rd
Savage Garden Rd
Glenstone Lodge
3.8 ★ (2361)
3-star hotel
Highland Rd
McCarter Rd
The Roaring Fork
Google
Keyboard shortcuts Map data ©2024 Google Terms

SCAN THE QR CODE

1. Open your device camera app.
2. Position the QR code in the camera frame.
3. Hold your phone steady.
4. Wait for the code to be recognized.
5. Once recognized, tap on the notification or follow the prompt to access the content or action associated with the Qr code

If you're looking for affordable yet spacious accommodations, Gatlinburg Town Square by Exploria Resorts offers comfortable rooms and suites with easy access to downtown Gatlinburg. This resort is particularly well-suited for families and longer stays due to its spacious layouts and kitchen facilities.

Key Features:

- **Rates:** Rooms start at around $80-$100 per night, making this a budget-friendly choice for families or those staying several nights.
- **Amenities:** Guests have access to both indoor and outdoor pools, hot tubs, and a fitness centre. The resort also features some rooms with fully equipped kitchens, allowing guests to save on dining costs by preparing their own meals.
- **Location:** Located just a short walk from the Parkway, it offers a mix of convenience and comfort for guests looking to be near the action without spending too much.

You can learn more and make reservations at [Gatlinburg Town Square by Exploria](https://www.exploriaresorts.com/gatlinburg-town-square/).

3. Sleep Inn & Suites Gatlinburg

For those seeking affordable accommodations with added comforts, Sleep Inn & Suites Gatlinburg is a great choice. Located just off the main strip, it's quiet but still close enough to all of the attractions you'd want to explore.

Key Features:

- **Rates:** Prices start from $75 per night, making it a solid choice for budget-conscious travellers.
- **Amenities:** Guests enjoy amenities such as an indoor heated pool with a lazy river and hot tub, free Wi-Fi, and complimentary breakfast each morning.
- **Family-Friendly:** The rooms are well-suited for families, with options for suites that provide extra space and comfort.

More details and booking options are available at [Sleep Inn Gatlinburg](https://www.choicehotels.com/sleep-inn).

4. Baymont by Wyndham Gatlinburg on the River

Baymont by Wyndham is a great option for travellers seeking a clean and comfortable stay without spending too much. Positioned along the Little Pigeon River, Baymont offers scenic river views and easy access to the Parkway.

Key Features:

- **Rates:** Rooms typically start at around $85 per night, with seasonal variations.
- **Amenities:** The hotel offers a free continental breakfast, indoor pool, fitness centre, and rooms that include a private balcony overlooking the river—perfect for enjoying the sound of flowing water after a day of exploration.
- **Pet-Friendly:** For those travelling with pets, Baymont welcomes your furry friends, which is great for making your vacation complete.

For bookings and more information, visit [Baymont by Wyndham Gatlinburg](https://www.wyndhamhotels.com/baymont).

5. Microtel Inn & Suites by Wyndham Gatlinburg

For travellers who just need a clean, simple place to sleep and don't plan to spend much time in their hotel, Microtel Inn & Suites is a budget-friendly option that offers a comfortable stay.

Key Features:

- **Rates:** Starting as low as $60 per night, it's one of the most affordable options in Gatlinburg.
- **Amenities:** While not as luxurious as other options, Microtel provides everything needed for a comfortable stay, including free Wi-Fi, complimentary breakfast, and air-conditioned rooms.
- **Location:** It's just a short walk to downtown Gatlinburg, allowing you to easily access shops, restaurants, and attractions.

To learn more or make a reservation, check out [Microtel Gatlinburg](https://www.wyndhamhotels.com/microtel).

Tips for Budget Accommodation in Gatlinburg

- **Book Early:** Gatlinburg is a popular tourist destination, and rooms at budget-friendly hotels tend to fill up quickly, especially during peak seasons like summer and fall. Book well in advance to secure the best rates.

- **Travel Off-Season:** Visiting during the off-peak months (such as winter, excluding the holiday season) can help you save a significant amount on accommodation.
- **Consider Weekdays:** If possible, book your stay during the week instead of weekends. Weekday rates are generally lower, and you'll also experience less crowded attractions.
- **Look for Package Deals:** Many hotels in Gatlinburg offer package deals that include tickets to local attractions, which can save you both time and money.

C. Luxury Stays with Scenic Views

1. The Lodge at Buckberry Creek

The Lodge at Buckberry Creek

The Lodge At Buckberry Creek
961 Campbell Lead Rd, Gatlinburg, TN 37738, United States
4.6
View larger map
Directions

Ski Mountain Chalet Rentals
Campbell Lead Rd
Campbell
The Lodge At Buckberry Creek
4.6 (137)
4-star hotel
Wiley Oakley Dr
Chalet Village
Ski Mountain Rd
Google
Keyboard shortcuts Map data ©2024 Google Terms

SCAN THE QR CODE

1. Open your device camera app.
2. Position the QR code in the camera frame.
3. Hold your phone steady.
4. Wait for the code to be recognized.
5. Once recognized, tap on the notification or follow the prompt to access the content or action associated with the Qr code

Nestled in the heart of the Smokies, The Lodge at Buckberry Creek offers a serene mountain retreat for those seeking luxury in the midst of nature. The lodge is set on over 26 acres of beautiful woodland, with views that showcase the rolling hills of the Smoky Mountains.

Key Features:

- **Scenic Views:** Each suite and room at Buckberry Lodge comes with a private balcony that opens up to stunning mountain vistas, making it ideal for those who wish to take in the beauty of nature without leaving their room.
- **Gourmet Dining:** The lodge offers fine dining with a menu that features locally-sourced Appalachian cuisine, served in a rustic yet elegant setting. Imagine enjoying a delicious dinner while watching the sunset over the mountains.
- **Rustic Charm with Modern Luxury:** Rooms are equipped with luxurious amenities, including fireplaces and spacious bathtubs for soaking away the day's adventures.

Rates at The Lodge at Buckberry Creek start from $300 per night. It is a perfect destination for romantic getaways or for anyone wanting to disconnect and recharge in a luxurious mountain setting. You can find more details at [Buckberry Lodge](https://buckberrylodge.com).

2. Riverstone Resort & Spa

Riverstone Resort & Spa

Riverstone Resort & Spa

212 Dollywood Ln, Pigeon Forge, TN 37868, United States

4.5

Directions

View larger map

Pigeon Forge Chamber of Commerce

Dollywood Ln

Riverstone Resort & Spa
4.5 ★ (2028)
4-star hotel

Toy Box Mini Golf
Miniature golf course

TopJump Trampoline & Extreme Arena
Trampoline park, VR games & concessions

Best Western Plaza Inn
4.3 ★ (2621)

Trout House 350

Google

Keyboard shortcuts Map data ©2024 Google Terms

SCAN THE QR CODE

1. Open your device camera app.
2. Position the QR code in the camera frame.
3. Hold your phone steady.
4. Wait for the code to be recognized.
5. Once recognized, tap on the notification or follow the prompt to access the content or action associated with the Qr code

Riverstone Resort & Spa is one of Gatlinburg's most popular high-end accommodations, offering a luxurious blend of natural beauty and modern comfort. Located just outside of Gatlinburg, this resort features spacious condos and is perfect for families or couples who want a more private and upscale experience.

Key Features:

- **Spa and Wellness:** The resort offers a full-service spa, perfect for unwinding after a long day of exploring. Guests can indulge in massages, facials, and other treatments designed to rejuvenate both the body and mind.
- **Luxurious Condos:** Each condo features premium bedding, large living areas, full kitchens, and private balconies overlooking either the golf course or the Little Pigeon River, providing breathtaking views of the Smoky Mountains.
- **Amenities for All:** The resort offers an indoor pool, a lazy river, and a fitness centre, making it a great choice for those who want the luxury of a spa with the amenities of a resort.

Rates typically start from $250 per night and vary depending on the size and amenities of the condo.

To make a reservation, visit [Riverstone Resort & Spa](https://www.riverstoneresort.com).

3. Margaritaville Resort Gatlinburg

If you're looking for a luxurious stay with a bit of a playful twist, Margaritaville Resort in Gatlinburg combines a relaxing, tropical vibe with the charm of the Smoky Mountains. Located downtown, this upscale resort is perfect for those who want to blend luxury and adventure during their stay.

Key Features:

- **Tropical Luxury:** Rooms and suites are designed to evoke a relaxed, island-style getaway with plush bedding, private balconies, and luxurious showers.
- **St. Somewhere Spa:** The resort features an exclusive spa where guests can indulge in massages, manicures, and other treatments designed for ultimate relaxation.
- **Central Location:** Margaritaville Resort is located downtown, providing guests with quick and easy access to local shops, restaurants, and entertainment venues.

Prices start from $220 to $350 per night, depending on the room type and season. It’s an ideal spot for those wanting to mix the lively atmosphere of

Gatlinburg with high-end relaxation. Book your stay at [Margaritaville Gatlinburg](https://www.margaritavilleresorts.com/margaritaville-resort-gatlinburg).

4. Greystone Lodge on the River

For those wanting a combination of scenic views, comfort, and luxury, Greystone Lodge on the River provides an excellent choice. Situated along the Little Pigeon River, this lodge is not only close to downtown attractions but also offers stunning river views that create a peaceful, calming atmosphere.

Key Features:

- **Riverside Rooms:** Many rooms at Greystone Lodge have private balconies that overlook the river, giving guests the opportunity to wake up to the sounds of flowing water. The rooms are spacious and furnished with upscale amenities.
- **Location:** The lodge is centrally located, allowing easy access to popular spots like Ripley's Aquarium of the Smokies and Ober Gatlinburg without the need for long commutes.
- **Family-Friendly Amenities:** The lodge includes a heated outdoor pool, making it a

great spot for families looking for comfort, style, and plenty of activities.

Room rates start from $220 per night, depending on the season and availability. More information is available at [Greystone Lodge](https://greystonelodgetn.com).

5. Treehouse Grove at Norton Creek

For a unique luxurious experience, Treehouse Grove at Norton Creek offers something truly special. Imagine staying in an elegantly designed treehouse elevated above the ground, providing breathtaking views of the surrounding forest.

Key Features:

- **Unique Stay:** Each treehouse is beautifully crafted, combining luxury with a sense of adventure. You'll have modern comforts like plush beds and beautiful decks, but you'll also be surrounded by the peace of nature.
- **Natural Setting:** Set among the trees, the views are unparalleled, and you'll have the chance to reconnect with nature. It's perfect for couples seeking a romantic escape or families looking for something different.
- **Amenities:** Every treehouse is equipped with air conditioning, a kitchenette, and

private decks. The environment blends luxury with nature, making it feel like you're in a secluded forest while still having access to all the comforts of a high-end retreat.

Prices start from $300 per night, making Treehouse Grove a perfect splurge for a memorable experience in the Smoky Mountains. You can learn more at [Treehouse Grove](https://www.treehousegrove.com).

D. Cabins and Unique Lodging Experiences

1. Cabins of the Smoky Mountains

Cabins of the Smoky Mountains is one of the largest cabin rental companies in the area, offering a wide variety of cabins suitable for couples, families, and even large groups. These cabins are located throughout the Smokies, with many offering stunning views, seclusion, and a rustic yet luxurious experience.

Key Features:

- **Range of Cabins:** From romantic one-bedroom cabins to large lodges that can accommodate up to 50 guests, Cabins of the

Smoky Mountains provides options for every type of traveller.

- **Amenities:** Many cabins come equipped with hot tubs, game rooms, home theatres, and fully equipped kitchens, giving guests everything they need for a comfortable stay. The wrap-around decks provide breathtaking views, especially during sunrise or sunset.
- **Secluded Locations:** Some cabins are nestled deep in the woods, providing peace and quiet, while others are closer to downtown for those who want to be near the action.

Rates for cabins vary widely depending on the size and season, ranging from $150 to $500 per night. You can find more information or book your stay at [Cabins of the Smoky Mountains](https://www.cabinsofthesmokymountains.com).

2. Elk Springs Resort

For those who are looking for a tranquil escape, Elk Springs Resort offers beautifully designed cabins that are perfect for unwinding after a day of adventure. Located just outside of downtown Gatlinburg, Elk Springs cabins are nestled among the trees, giving you the peaceful setting of a true Smoky Mountain retreat.

Key Features:

- **Unique Cabins:** Each cabin at Elk Springs is individually designed, offering different features, from large wrap-around decks to private hot tubs. The cabins have charming log interiors, with plenty of modern touches to keep you comfortable.
- **Amenities:** Cabins come with modern appliances, game rooms, and in some cases, home theatre systems. Many of them have spacious hot tubs on the decks, perfect for enjoying the crisp mountain air.
- **Privacy and Seclusion:** The cabins are located within a private resort area, which means you can enjoy a tranquil environment away from the hustle and bustle of downtown Gatlinburg.

Rates start from around $170 per night, depending on the type of cabin and season. More details are available at [Elk Springs Resort](https://www.elkspringsresort.com).

3. Treehouse Grove at Norton Creek

If you want to experience the Smokies from a different perspective, Treehouse Grove at Norton Creek provides a unique lodging option where you can literally sleep among the trees. These treehouses are beautifully crafted, with modern comforts in a secluded natural setting.

Key Features:

- **Unique Stay:** The treehouses are designed by "Treehouse Master" Pete Nelson and are crafted to blend seamlessly with the surrounding forest. Staying in one of these treehouses gives you an immersive experience with nature, while still providing the luxury of comfortable beds, stylish decor, and spacious decks.
- **Scenic Location:** Nestled among the trees near Norton Creek, these treehouses offer a perfect escape for those looking to unwind in nature. Each unit is raised high among the trees, providing a one-of-a-kind view of the forest.
- **Modern Amenities:** Despite being in the trees, each unit comes with air conditioning, a kitchenette, and comfortable living areas. It's ideal for couples or families wanting an out-of-the-ordinary stay.

Treehouse rates start from $300 per night, depending on availability and the season. Bookings and more information can be found at [Treehouse Grove](https://www.treehousegrove.com).

4. The Lodge at Hidden Mountain Resort

Hidden Mountain Resort offers a variety of cabins and lodges that are perfect for large families or groups. The cabins range from quaint and cosy units to larger, luxurious lodges that can accommodate big groups for family reunions or weddings.

Key Features:

- **Variety of Cabins:** Hidden Mountain Resort provides everything from smaller, intimate cabins for couples to massive lodges for groups of up to 20 people.
- **Rustic Luxury:** The cabins are well-equipped, featuring everything you need for a comfortable stay—full kitchens, spacious living areas, hot tubs, and large decks. Many cabins have fireplaces, perfect for warming up on a chilly mountain night.
- **On-Site Amenities:** The resort features walking trails, a fishing pond, and a pool for guests to enjoy. Hidden Mountain's location is secluded enough to be peaceful but close

enough to Gatlinburg that guests can easily venture into town for activities and dining.

Rates vary based on the size and season, ranging from $200 to $600 per night. Reservations can be made at [Hidden Mountain Resort](https://hiddenmountain.com).

5. Gatlinburg Falls Resort

Gatlinburg Falls Resort offers luxury cabins that provide a combination of rustic charm and modern luxury. This resort is known for its high-end cabins, offering guests privacy, spectacular views, and plenty of amenities to make their stay special.

Key Features:

- **Luxury Cabins:** Each cabin comes with log-inspired decor and plenty of luxury amenities. You'll find hot tubs, game rooms, and even theatre rooms in many of these properties. It's ideal for those looking to spend quality time with family or friends in a luxurious setting.
- **Location:** The resort is located just a short drive from downtown Gatlinburg, making it a convenient choice for those wanting easy access to both the national park and local attractions.

- **Scenic Views:** The cabins provide stunning views of the Smoky Mountains, whether you're relaxing on the deck, sitting in the hot tub, or enjoying a morning coffee by the fireplace.

Rates at Gatlinburg Falls Resort start from $200 per night, with larger luxury cabins reaching higher prices based on size and features. Book your stay through [Gatlinburg Falls Resort](https://gatlinburgfallsresort.com).

Chapter 4: Top Attractions and Things to Do

A. Great Smoky Mountains National Park

Welcome to Great Smoky Mountains National Park, a true treasure of nature that lies on the border between Tennessee and North Carolina, covering over 522,000 acres of breathtaking beauty. As the most visited national park in the United States, it draws millions of visitors every year with its stunning vistas, diverse wildlife, and rich cultural history. The park is open all year, and best of all, it's free to enter—though a small parking fee applies if you plan to stay longer than 15 minutes. The Smokies truly offer a slice of wilderness that's both accessible and deeply rewarding for all kinds of travelers.

History of the Park

The park has an inspiring history rooted in conservation. In 1934, Great Smoky Mountains National Park was established thanks to a mix of federal funding and private donations, with a significant contribution of $5 million from John D. Rockefeller. This vast tract of land was gradually pieced together from numerous private properties, ensuring that these beautiful mountains could be preserved for future generations. Over time, the park gained recognition as an International Biosphere Reserve in 1976 and became a UNESCO World Heritage Site in 1983, thanks to its ecological richness and cultural significance.

Getting There and Contact Information

The park is easily accessible from several locations:

- Sugarlands Visitor Center in Gatlinburg, Tennessee, is one of the main entry points and is just a short drive from downtown Gatlinburg. It provides maps, exhibits, and information to help you plan your visit.
- Oconaluftee Visitor Center near Cherokee, North Carolina, also serves as a major gateway into the park.

If you're flying in, the closest airports are:

- McGhee Tyson Airport (TYS) in Knoxville, about 50 miles from the park.

- Asheville Regional Airport (AVL) in North Carolina, approximately 55 miles away.

For further information, you can contact the park headquarters at (865) 436-1200 or visit their website at [Great Smoky Mountains National Park](https://www.nps.gov/grsm/planyourvisit/index.htm).

Things to Do in the Park

Great Smoky Mountains National Park offers endless activities for every type of adventurer:

1. Hiking: The park is home to over 800 miles of trails, ranging from easy family-friendly walks to challenging multi-day hikes. Popular trails include:

- **Alum Cave Trail:** This 5-mile round trip trail is famous for its natural beauty, featuring scenic views, an old-growth forest, and the impressive Arch Rock.
- **Laurel Falls Trail:** A 2.4-mile round trip hike that leads to a beautiful two-tiered waterfall. It's an ideal choice if you're looking for a shorter, but rewarding trek.

2. Clingmans Dome: At 6,643 feet, Clingmans Dome is the highest peak in the park and offers spectacular 360-degree views of the Smokies from an observation tower. On clear days, you can see up to 100 miles in every direction. The half-mile paved trail to the tower is steep, but the panoramic views are well worth the effort.

3. Scenic Drives: If hiking isn't your thing, take a scenic drive along Newfound Gap Road. This route cuts through the park from Gatlinburg to Cherokee and takes you past breathtaking vistas, forests, and mountain peaks. The drive offers many pull-off points where you can take photos or simply enjoy the views.

4. Cades Cove: One of the most popular spots in the park, Cades Cove is an 11-mile loop road that lets you explore a picturesque valley surrounded by mountains. This area is rich in history, with well-preserved pioneer structures, and is also a great place to spot wildlife, such as white-tailed deer and black bears.

5. Waterfalls and Nature Trails: The park is known for its many waterfalls, including Abrams Falls and Rainbow Falls. The trails leading to these waterfalls provide a chance to enjoy both the beauty of the cascades and the surrounding lush forest.

Where to Stay

The park offers a mix of accommodation options:

- **LeConte Lodge:** If you're seeking adventure, consider staying at LeConte Lodge, the only lodging available within the park. Built in 1926, the lodge is accessible only by hiking, making it an exclusive experience for those wanting to immerse themselves in nature. Supplies are brought in by llama trains, adding to the charm of the stay. Reservations fill quickly, so make sure to book well in advance through the [LeConte Lodge website](https://www.lecontelodge.com).
- **Nearby Towns:** Gatlinburg and Cherokee are great base towns for exploring the Smokies. They offer a range of hotels, cabins, and lodges that cater to different budgets.

What to Eat and Drink

There are no restaurants within the park itself, so it's important to pack a picnic or plan meals accordingly. Nearby towns such as Gatlinburg have plenty of dining options where you can enjoy everything from traditional Southern comfort food to international cuisine after a day in the park. You can also grab picnic supplies from local stores and enjoy a meal surrounded by nature at one of the many picnic areas throughout the park.

Costs and Best Time to Visit

- **Entry Fee:** One of the unique things about Great Smoky Mountains National Park is that it has no entrance fee. However, you will need to purchase a parking tag if you plan to park for more than 15 minutes, starting at $5 per day.
- **Best Time to Visit:** The summer and fall are the most popular times to visit. Summer is perfect for enjoying the park's lush greenery, while fall draws visitors with its stunning foliage. If you're looking to avoid crowds, winter is a peaceful time to visit, but be aware that some areas may be closed due to weather conditions.

Booking and Information

To make the most of your visit, consider checking the park's official website for alerts, maps, and updates: [Great Smoky Mountains National Park](https://www.nps.gov/grsm/planyourvisit/index.htm). The visitor centers are a great starting point for picking up maps, asking questions, and getting tips from park rangers.

B. Gatlinburg SkyLift and Space Needle

Gatlinburg's SkyLift and Space Needle are two of the town's most iconic attractions, offering you spectacular views of the Smoky Mountains from breathtaking perspectives. These attractions will give you a bird's-eye view of the natural beauty that surrounds Gatlinburg, making them perfect for visitors who want to experience the magic of the Smokies from above.

Gatlinburg SkyLift Park

The Gatlinburg SkyLift is one of Gatlinburg's oldest and most loved attractions, first opening in 1954. The SkyLift takes you up Crockett Mountain, providing stunning views along the way, and brings you to the top, where you can explore the SkyLift Park. Once you reach the top, you'll be greeted with an incredible panoramic view of Gatlinburg, framed by the majestic Smoky Mountains.

What to Do at SkyLift Park:

- **SkyBridge:** The highlight of your SkyLift experience is walking across the Gatlinburg SkyBridge. This is the longest pedestrian suspension bridge in North America, stretching 680 feet across a beautiful valley. The glass-floor sections in the middle of the bridge are a thrill—you can look straight down at the scenery below, making it both exciting and slightly nerve-wracking.
- **SkyDeck and SkyCenter:** After crossing the bridge, relax on the SkyDeck and enjoy the views from a different perspective. The SkyCenter offers a place to grab a snack, a drink, or a souvenir to remember your adventure.
- **Night Visits:** SkyLift Park is also open after dark, giving you the opportunity to see Gatlinburg lit up against the night sky. The SkyBridge lights up in the evening, adding a magical touch to your experience.

Cost and Booking:

- Tickets for the SkyLift are $34.95 for adults and $20.95 for children. Seniors and veterans may qualify for discounts, and it's recommended to book tickets online in advance to save time and guarantee your spot.

- The SkyLift Park is open year-round, weather permitting, from 9:00 a.m. to 10:00 p.m. during peak season, but hours vary in winter months.

For more information or to book tickets, visit [Gatlinburg SkyLift Park](https://www.gatlinburgskylift.com).

Gatlinburg Space Needle

Another way to take in the beauty of Gatlinburg is by visiting the Gatlinburg Space Needle, a 407-foot-tall observation tower located in the heart of downtown. Built in 1969, the Space Needle offers spectacular 360-degree views of Gatlinburg and the surrounding Smoky Mountains. The tower is accessible by glass elevators that take you to the observation deck, giving you a bird's-eye view of everything from the bustling streets of Gatlinburg to the rolling green mountains beyond.

What to Do at the Space Needle:

- **Observation Deck:** The main attraction of the Space Needle is, of course, the observation deck. From here, you can use viewfinders to get a closer look at the surrounding area, including Mount LeConte and other peaks in the Smoky Mountains.

- **Arcadia:** At the base of the Space Needle, you'll find Arcadia, a large amusement center with arcade games and other entertainment options for families and kids. It's a great way to spend some time after enjoying the views from above.
- **Educational Aspects:** The Space Needle also offers educational exhibits on the history of Gatlinburg and the Smoky Mountains, adding a layer of context and appreciation for what you're seeing from the observation deck.

Cost and Booking:

- Tickets for the Space Needle are $15 for adults and $9 for children, with discounts available for groups.
- The Space Needle is open year-round, generally from 10:00 a.m. until midnight, allowing you to visit during the day or experience the magic of seeing Gatlinburg lit up at night.

For more details, visit [Gatlinburg Space Needle](https://www.gatlinburgspaceneedle.com).

How to Reach These Attractions

Both the SkyLift and the Space Needle are located in downtown Gatlinburg, making them easily accessible from most of the lodging options in the area. If you're staying in downtown Gatlinburg, you can simply walk to these attractions, as they're centrally located along the Gatlinburg Parkway. Alternatively, if you're staying a bit farther out, the Gatlinburg Trolley offers convenient stops near these attractions, providing a stress-free way to get around.

Best Time to Visit

The best time to visit the SkyLift or Space Needle depends on the kind of views you want:

- Summer provides lush green views of the mountains, and everything is alive and vibrant.
- Fall is the most popular time to visit, as the Smokies explode with colour, turning the views from the SkyLift and Space Needle into breathtaking works of art.
- Winter is ideal if you love snow-capped mountains and want a quieter experience without the crowds.
- Night Visits to both attractions are highly recommended, especially during the holidays when Gatlinburg is beautifully decorated with lights.

Dining Nearby

After enjoying the views, you'll likely be ready to grab a bite to eat. Downtown Gatlinburg has plenty of options, from local Southern cuisine to international flavours. Some great places to check out nearby include:

- The Peddler Steakhouse for a classic Gatlinburg dining experience right by the river.
- Smoky Mountain Brewery if you're looking for something casual with local brews.
- Bubba Gump Shrimp Co. is another fun option for seafood lovers, especially if you want a family-friendly atmosphere.

C. Ripley's Aquarium of the Smokies

Description and Highlights

Ripley's Aquarium opened in 2000 and has since become one of the most popular attractions in

Gatlinburg. It houses over 10,000 exotic sea creatures spread across 350 different species, offering you a chance to see everything from the graceful movements of stingrays to the sharp teeth of sharks. The aquarium is divided into multiple themed exhibits that take you through different marine environments.

Highlights of the Aquarium:

- **Shark Lagoon:** One of the most popular exhibits, the Shark Lagoon offers a walk-through tunnel with a moving sidewalk, giving you a 360-degree view of the underwater world. You'll feel like you're part of the ocean as sharks, sea turtles, and rays swim around and above you.
- **Penguin Playhouse:** The Penguin Playhouse is another major highlight, especially for families. It features African penguins in an environment where they can swim, slide, and waddle around. The viewing tunnels allow kids and adults alike to get up close and personal with these charming creatures.
- **Touch-a-Ray Bay:** In this interactive exhibit, you can gently touch the backs of stingrays as they glide gracefully through the water. It's a wonderful opportunity to

interact with these creatures in a safe and controlled environment.

- **Discovery Center:** The Discovery Center offers hands-on learning opportunities for children and adults. There are educational activities, touch tanks, and plenty of fascinating facts about the marine animals.

Costs and Booking

Tickets for Ripley's Aquarium are $39.99 for adults and $24.99 for children (ages 6-11), while kids under 5 are free. You can save a few dollars by purchasing your tickets online in advance. The aquarium also offers combo tickets that include other Ripley's attractions, allowing you to enjoy multiple experiences for a discounted price.

Ripley's Aquarium is open 365 days a year, with varying hours. During peak seasons like summer and holidays, it's open from 9:00 a.m. to 10:00 p.m.. In off-peak months, it usually closes earlier, around 8:00 p.m. It's best to check their official website for up-to-date hours and to book your tickets in advance: [Ripley's Aquarium Gatlinburg](https://www.ripleyaquariums.com/gatlinburg/).

What to Expect During Your Visit

Ripley's Aquarium of the Smokies is designed to be immersive, educational, and fun. Whether you're fascinated by the creatures that live in coral reefs, curious about the mysteries of the ocean depths, or just love penguins, there is something here for everyone. Plan to spend around two to three hours exploring the different exhibits and participating in the interactive activities.

If you want to elevate your experience, Ripley's offers a variety of special experiences, such as:

- **Penguin Encounter:** Get up close and personal with the penguins, learn about their behavior, and even take a photo with them.
- **Sleep with the Sharks:** Spend the night in the Shark Lagoon tunnel! This is a special overnight program that gives you the chance to sleep beneath the ocean's predators and learn more about marine life.

For those looking for a more in-depth experience, Ripley's also offers behind-the-scenes tours that take you to areas usually off-limits to visitors. These tours show you how the aquarium operates, including animal care, feeding, and water maintenance systems.

Dining and Shopping

There's a convenient café within the aquarium if you're feeling hungry during your visit. The café offers snacks, beverages, and light meals, perfect for refueling before continuing your adventure. Additionally, there's a gift shop near the exit where you can pick up a souvenir to remember your visit. From plush marine animals to T-shirts, you're bound to find something to take home with you.

How to Reach Ripley's Aquarium

Ripley's Aquarium of the Smokies is centrally located in downtown Gatlinburg, making it easily accessible for most visitors. If you're staying in a hotel in Gatlinburg, you can simply walk to the aquarium. Alternatively, you can take the Gatlinburg Trolley, which has multiple stops near the aquarium. Parking is available near the aquarium, though it can be limited, especially during peak times. It's advisable to arrive early or consider parking in one of the nearby public parking lots.

Best Time to Visit

- Mornings tend to be the least crowded, especially on weekdays, so visiting early in the day is your best chance to avoid long lines.

- The fall season is particularly beautiful, as you can combine your visit to Ripley's with a walk around Gatlinburg when the town is blanketed in gorgeous fall colors.
- Winter holidays also bring a festive atmosphere, with Gatlinburg decked out in lights and decorations, making your visit extra special.

Nearby Attractions

Ripley's Aquarium is just one of several attractions in downtown Gatlinburg. After your visit, you might want to check out:

- Ripley's Believe It or Not! Odditorium, featuring strange and quirky exhibits.
- Anakeesta for a mountaintop experience and more incredible views of the Smokies.
- Gatlinburg SkyLift Park is also within walking distance, making it easy to include multiple attractions in your day.

D. Ober Gatlinburg Amusement Park and Ski Resort

If you're looking for a mix of adventure, breathtaking views, and year-round fun, then Ober Gatlinburg Amusement Park and Ski Resort is the place to be. This iconic attraction combines an amusement park, ski slopes, and a wildlife encounter all in one spot, making it an ideal destination for families, couples, or anyone craving a day packed with activities. From thrilling rides to winter sports, Ober Gatlinburg offers something exciting in every season.

Description and History

Ober Gatlinburg has been a staple of the Gatlinburg experience since 1962, when it first opened as a ski resort. It has since expanded into a full-blown amusement park with a variety of attractions suitable for all ages. Located just above downtown Gatlinburg, it's easily accessible via the Aerial Tramway, which takes you on a scenic journey up the mountainside. Ober Gatlinburg's name, derived from a German word meaning "upper" or "above," fits perfectly for this mountaintop oasis.

How to Get There

Getting to Ober Gatlinburg is half the fun. The Aerial Tramway, which departs from downtown Gatlinburg (located at 1001 Parkway), offers a spectacular two-mile ride up to the resort. It's one of the largest aerial tramways in America, capable of holding up to 120 passengers, and it provides stunning views of the Smoky Mountains along the way. The tram runs daily, and tickets cost $19 for adults and $15 for children. If you'd rather drive, there's also a winding scenic road that leads to the resort, and parking is available for $10 per vehicle.

For more details on tickets, tramway schedules, and directions, visit [Ober Gatlinburg's official website](https://obergatlinburg.com).

Things to Do at Ober Gatlinburg

Ober Gatlinburg offers activities throughout the year, with options changing as the seasons do. Whether you're visiting in the summer or winter, you're sure to find something to love.

Winter Activities

- **Skiing and Snowboarding:** Ober Gatlinburg is the only ski resort in Tennessee. During the winter months, it offers skiing, snowboarding, and snow tubing. With nine ski trails ranging from beginner to advanced, it's perfect for all skill levels. If you're new to skiing or snowboarding, lessons are available, and you can also rent all necessary gear on-site.
- **Snow Tubing:** Snow tubing is one of the most popular activities, offering fun for all ages. The tubing sessions last about 90 minutes and must be booked in advance, as spots fill quickly.

Year-Round Activities

- **Aerial Tramway and Scenic Chairlift:** The Aerial Tramway and Scenic Chairlift are two great ways to take in the surrounding mountain views. The Scenic Chairlift takes you to the highest point in Gatlinburg and offers breathtaking views of the Smokies, especially during fall when the leaves are ablaze in vibrant colors.
- **Alpine Slide:** If you're visiting in the warmer months, the Alpine Slide is a thrilling ride that takes you down a 1,800-foot track on a wheeled sled. It's a

great mix of speed and scenery as you zip down the mountain.

- **Mountain Coaster:** For adrenaline lovers, the Mountain Coaster is a must. This gravity-propelled coaster lets you control the speed as you race down the mountainside, with views of the Smokies adding to the thrill.

Wildlife Encounter

For a more relaxed experience, visit Ober's Wildlife Encounter. You'll find native animals like black bears, river otters, bobcats, and more. This small zoo provides an up-close look at some of the species native to the Smoky Mountains and offers an educational experience for visitors of all ages.

Ice Skating and Other Indoor Fun

Ober Gatlinburg also features a year-round indoor ice rink where you can enjoy skating regardless of the weather outside. Skating tickets cost about $12 per person, including skate rental. The indoor area also offers arcade games and a variety of shops, making it a great place to hang out, especially on a rainy day.

Dining at Ober Gatlinburg

After a day full of activities, you're bound to work up an appetite. Seasons of Ober Restaurant offers a casual dining experience with a menu that features classic American cuisine like burgers, sandwiches, salads, and hearty comfort food. It's an ideal spot for lunch or dinner while enjoying spectacular views from the mountaintop.

If you're in the mood for a quick snack, The Market offers lighter options like pretzels, popcorn, and hot beverages—perfect for warming up after a chilly winter adventure. There's also the Sidewalk Café, which offers a variety of fast food items and sweet treats.

Costs and Booking

- **Aerial Tramway:** $19 for adults and $15 for children.
- **Ski Lift Tickets:** Prices vary depending on the season and time of day, with full-day lift tickets typically costing around $50-$70.
- **Snow Tubing:** Tickets are approximately $30 per person, and advance reservations are strongly recommended, especially during peak times.
- **Mountain Coaster:** Rides cost $16 per person, with discounts available for additional rides.

Tickets for most activities can be purchased online at [Ober Gatlinburg](https://obergatlinburg.com). Buying tickets in advance is highly recommended, especially during the peak seasons of summer and winter when the resort is busiest.

Best Time to Visit

Winter is a fantastic time to visit Ober Gatlinburg if you're interested in skiing, snowboarding, or snow tubing. The slopes are busiest from December to February, and the festive winter decorations make for a magical experience.

- Summer offers a completely different vibe. The weather is warm, the trails are accessible, and all the amusement rides are open, making it ideal for families looking for a mix of adventure and scenic views.
- Fall is perhaps the most beautiful time to visit. The entire Smoky Mountains region bursts into fiery reds, oranges, and yellows, making the rides and chairlifts even more spectacular.

Where to Stay

While Ober Gatlinburg itself does not offer on-site lodging, you'll find plenty of accommodation options in downtown Gatlinburg, just a short tram ride away. Whether you're looking for a luxurious stay, a family-friendly hotel, or a cozy cabin, Gatlinburg has a wide range of places to suit every need.

E. Local Artisans and Craftsmen

One of the most rewarding experiences when visiting Gatlinburg is exploring the vibrant local artisan community. Gatlinburg is home to the Great Smoky Arts & Crafts Community, a group of talented craftsmen and women who work tirelessly to keep Appalachian culture and heritage alive. This eight-mile loop, just outside of downtown Gatlinburg, is a haven for those who appreciate art, craftsmanship, and locally made goods. Here, you can watch artisans at work, learn about traditional crafts, and pick up unique souvenirs that carry a piece of the Smoky Mountains' soul.

Great Smoky Arts & Crafts Community

The Great Smoky Arts & Crafts Community is the largest group of independent artisans in North America, and it was established in 1937. This community is located along an eight-mile loop on Glades Road, just a few miles from downtown Gatlinburg. The artisans in this community continue to use traditional methods to produce everything from pottery and paintings to wood carvings and handwoven baskets. Visiting the community is like stepping into a living museum where you can watch artists in action, learn about their processes, and even try your hand at making something yourself.

Types of Crafts and Artisans You'll Find

The Great Smoky Arts & Crafts Community is home to dozens of studios, galleries, and shops that offer a wide range of handmade items. Whether you're interested in something rustic, artistic, or functional, you'll find it here. Here are some of the crafts you can expect to find:

- **Pottery:** Many artisans in the community create beautiful, handcrafted pottery pieces, from bowls and mugs to decorative sculptures. One notable potter is Alewine Pottery, which is known for its unique glazes and rustic, nature-inspired designs.

- **Wood Carving:** Wood carving is another popular craft in the Smokies, and you can find everything from detailed animal figurines to large pieces of furniture. The woodworkers often use local hardwoods like walnut and cherry, which add a special touch to each piece.
- **Weaving and Basketry:** Handwoven baskets and textiles are a significant part of the Appalachian tradition. Many artisans use traditional weaving methods to create durable, functional baskets and intricate quilts that tell stories of the Smoky Mountains.
- **Glass Blowing:** Some studios offer live glass-blowing demonstrations, where you can see artisans shape and mold molten glass into beautiful decorative items and jewelry.
- **Painting and Sculpture:** The artistic spirit of the Smokies is also evident in the many painters and sculptors who capture the breathtaking landscapes of the area. Many local painters use vibrant colors to recreate the beauty of the mountains, especially the rich hues of fall.

What to Expect During Your Visit

Exploring the Arts & Crafts Community is a leisurely experience, as you stroll from shop to shop along the loop. Each artisan has a unique story, and most are happy to talk to you about their craft, how they learned it, and what inspires their work. The atmosphere is friendly and welcoming, and it's easy to spend several hours browsing, chatting with the artisans, and finding that perfect piece to take home as a reminder of your visit.

If you're interested in a more hands-on experience, some studios even offer workshops and classes, where you can try your hand at pottery, painting, or another craft. These experiences give you a chance to create something personal while learning from the experts.

Dining and Refreshments Along the Loop

You'll find several places along the Arts & Crafts Loop where you can stop for a meal or a snack. The Wild Plum Tea Room is a charming spot for lunch, offering homemade soups, sandwiches, and desserts. It's an ideal place to take a break from shopping and relax with a cup of tea. If you're looking for something a bit heartier, **Three Jimmy's** offers traditional Southern comfort food and is located just a short drive from the arts and crafts community.

Cost and Booking Information

The Arts & Crafts Community is open year-round, and there is no admission fee to visit the loop. Each shop is independently owned, so prices vary depending on the type of craft and the artist. Items range from affordable small souvenirs like handmade soaps or candles, to larger, more elaborate pieces such as paintings, sculptures, and furniture.

While many of the artisans have websites where you can view their work, the best way to experience the Arts & Crafts Community is in person, where you can see the craftsmanship up close and speak directly with the creators. If you're interested in taking a workshop, it's a good idea to call ahead to reserve your spot. You can find more information about the community and the artisans at [Great Smoky Arts & Crafts Community](https://www.gatlinburgcrafts.com).

Best Time to Visit

The Arts & Crafts Community is open throughout the year, but visiting in the fall is particularly special, as the loop is surrounded by the beautiful colors of the Smoky Mountains during this season.

Weekdays tend to be less crowded than weekends, giving you more time to talk to the artisans and enjoy demonstrations. The community also holds several arts and crafts shows throughout the year, particularly during the holidays, which are a great opportunity to see a wide variety of crafts in one place.

Nearby Attractions

The Arts & Crafts Community is not far from other popular Gatlinburg attractions:

- After visiting the artisans, consider heading into downtown Gatlinburg to explore more shops, restaurants, and attractions like Ripley's Aquarium of the Smokies or the Gatlinburg Space Needle.
- If you're in the mood for nature, the Great Smoky Mountains National Park is just a short drive away, offering hiking, scenic drives, and more outdoor adventure.

Flowers

Chapter 5: Outdoor Adventures

A. Hiking Trails for All Skill Levels

Gatlinburg, nestled next to the Great Smoky Mountains National Park, is a dream for hikers of all levels. Whether you're new to hiking or a seasoned trekker, the Smokies have a trail suited for you. And the best part? Most of the trails in the park are free to access, though you'll need to purchase a parking tag for $5 per day, $15 for a week, or $40 annually if you plan to park for more than 15 minutes. Below, we outline trails for beginners, moderate hikers, and experienced adventurers.

Easy Trails

For an easy introduction to hiking in the Smokies, Laurel Falls Trail is a fantastic choice. This 2.4-mile round-trip trail is paved and takes you to one of the most beautiful and easily accessible waterfalls in the park—Laurel Falls. Because it's paved, it's suitable for families with young children and strollers. During peak season, this trail can get busy, so visiting early in the morning or late in the afternoon is advisable. There's no cost for hiking the trail, but remember to pay the parking fee.

Another good beginner-friendly option is the Gatlinburg Trail, starting at the Sugarlands Visitor Center near Gatlinburg. This 3.8-mile round-trip path runs along the Little Pigeon River and offers easy, scenic views of the river and remnants of old homesteads. This trail is one of only two trails in the park that permits both dogs and bicycles, making it perfect for families and pet owners. Parking at Sugarlands Visitor Center is also covered under the park's $5 parking pass.

Moderate Trails

For those seeking a bit more adventure, Alum Cave Trail is an excellent choice. The trail is 5 miles round-trip to the Alum Cave Bluffs, which provide sweeping views of the Smoky Mountains. The path takes you through several interesting geological formations, including Arch Rock and Inspiration Point, before reaching the bluffs. The moderate difficulty makes this hike suitable for those with some hiking experience. The Alum Cave parking area also requires a parking pass, which you can easily purchase online at [Recreation.gov](https://www.recreation.gov/).

Another moderate option is the Abrams Falls Trail, located in Cades Cove. This trail is 5 miles round-trip and leads to the beautiful Abrams Falls, known for its powerful flow and stunning pool at the bottom. While the falls themselves are only about 20 feet high, the volume of water cascading down is impressive. The hike offers diverse scenery, including streams and lush forests, making it a favorite for hikers. The Cades Cove area is also covered by the parking pass system.

Challenging Trails

For experienced hikers, the Chimney Tops Trail provides a thrilling challenge. This 4-mile round-trip hike is steep, with an elevation gain of more than 1,400 feet. The last section of the hike includes a rock scramble, and while it's tough, the reward is absolutely worth it—a stunning view of the surrounding peaks and valleys of the Smokies. This hike is quite popular, so arriving early to secure parking is recommended. The trailhead for Chimney Tops requires a $5 parking pass as well.

If you're up for an all-day adventure, consider hiking to Mount LeConte via the Alum Cave Trail.

This hike is 11 miles round-trip and takes you to one of the highest peaks in the Smoky Mountains, Mount LeConte at 6,593 feet. The trail passes through various ecosystems, including lush forests, narrow ledges, and beautiful viewpoints. You can even spend the night at LeConte Lodge if you make a reservation well in advance—it's the only accommodation inside the park, and it fills up quickly.

Additional Costs and Permits

While there is no entrance fee for Great Smoky Mountains National Park, you are required to purchase a "Park It Forward" parking tag if you're staying at any parking area for more than 15 minutes. Tags can be purchased online or at the visitor centers within the park:

- $5 per day
- $15 for a week
- $40 for an annual pass

For backcountry camping, you'll also need a permit, which costs $8 per person per night and can be reserved on [Recreation.gov](https://www.recreation.gov/). It's always advisable to check trail conditions and parking availability ahead of time, especially for popular trails.

B. Waterfalls and Scenic Drives

Let's explore some of the best waterfalls and scenic drives that await you in Gatlinburg.

Waterfalls to Explore

The Smoky Mountains are dotted with picturesque waterfalls, each one offering its own unique charm. Whether you're up for a challenging hike to reach a secluded fall or want an easy walk, there's an adventure here for everyone.

Laurel Falls

Laurel Falls is one of the most popular and accessible waterfalls in the park. The Laurel Falls Trail is a 2.4-mile round-trip paved path that leads to a stunning 80-foot two-tiered waterfall. The trail is relatively easy, making it a favorite for families and casual hikers. Laurel Falls is especially beautiful during the spring and summer when the surrounding mountain laurel is in bloom. Because this trail is so popular, it's best to visit early in the morning or late in the afternoon to avoid the crowds. There's no cost to access the trail, but don't forget the $5 parking pass.

Abrams Falls

Located in Cades Cove, Abrams Falls is another must-see waterfall in the Smokies. This 20-foot waterfall may not be the tallest in the park, but its impressive flow rate and the large pool at its base make it a favorite. The Abrams Falls Trail is a 5-mile round-trip hike, rated as moderate due to some uneven terrain and elevation changes. The trail offers beautiful scenery along Abrams Creek, and the waterfall itself is a perfect spot for photos or a picnic. To reach the trailhead, you'll need to drive the Cades Cove Loop Road, which is itself a scenic drive that offers numerous opportunities to spot wildlife. There's no fee to hike Abrams Falls, but a $5 parking fee applies at the Cades Cove area.

Rainbow Falls

Rainbow Falls is the tallest single-drop waterfall in the park, cascading over **80 feet into the creek below. Named for the rainbow that appears in the mist on sunny afternoons, Rainbow Falls is a spectacular sight, especially after a heavy rain. The trail is 5.4 miles round-trip and is considered moderately difficult due to its length and elevation gain. It's a popular trail for hikers looking for a bit of a challenge, and the effort is rewarded by the stunning view at the end.

Scenic Drives

If hiking isn't your preference or if you simply want to take in the beauty of the Smokies from the comfort of your car, there are several scenic drives that offer incredible views of the landscape.

Newfound Gap Road

The Newfound Gap Road is one of the most famous scenic drives in the Smoky Mountains. Stretching 33 miles from Gatlinburg, Tennessee, to Cherokee, North Carolina, this route takes you through some of the park's most breathtaking landscapes. The road climbs from an elevation of 1,300 feet to 5,046 feet, offering sweeping views of the mountains and valleys below. There are plenty of pull-offs along the way, including Newfound Gap Overlook itself, which is the only place in the park where you can see into both Tennessee and North Carolina. The drive is completely free, and it's open year-round, though parts may close during winter due to weather conditions.

Cades Cove Loop Road

The Cades Cove Loop Road is a 11-mile one-way loop that winds through one of the most picturesque valleys in the Smokies. This drive offers not only stunning views of the mountains but also opportunities to see wildlife such as deer, wild turkeys, and even black bears. The loop road also passes by several historic buildings, including old churches, cabins, and barns, giving you a glimpse into the life of early settlers. The road can be crowded, especially during peak season, but it's well worth the time. Bicycles are also allowed on the loop, and on Wednesdays from May to September, the road is closed to motor vehicles, making it perfect for cyclists and pedestrians. As with all parts of the park, you will need a $5 parking tag if you stop along the route.

Roaring Fork Motor Nature Trail

If you're looking for a scenic drive that's a bit more off the beaten path, the Roaring Fork Motor Nature Trail is a fantastic choice. This 5.5-mile one-way loop takes you deep into the forest, passing by beautiful streams, old-growth trees, and historic cabins. Along the way, you'll find several trailheads, including the Trillium Gap Trail, which leads to Grotto Falls—the only waterfall in the park that you can actually walk behind. The road is narrow and winding, making it suitable only for cars (no RVs or trailers), and is typically open from mid-March through late November.

Tips for Visiting Waterfalls and Scenic Drives

- **Timing:** Visiting early in the morning is the best way to avoid crowds, especially during peak seasons like summer and fall. Additionally, early morning and late afternoon provide the best lighting for photographs.
- **Parking:** Make sure you have your $5 parking pass visible on your vehicle dashboard. You can purchase this pass at visitor centers or online through the [Great Smoky Mountains National Park website](https://www.nps.gov/grsm/planyourvisit/fees.htm).
- **Weather Considerations:** Be mindful of weather conditions. Roads and trails can close during heavy rain or snow, especially in winter. Always check the park's website for the latest updates on road and trail closures.

C. Whitewater Rafting and Ziplining

Whitewater Rafting in the Smokies

Whitewater rafting in the Smokies is an experience unlike any other, allowing you to get up close and personal with the wild and beautiful waterways of the region. The Pigeon River, located just a short drive from Gatlinburg, is one of the most popular places for rafting adventures.

The Pigeon River Experience

The Pigeon River runs through Hartford, Tennessee, about a 30-minute drive from Gatlinburg, and is divided into two sections: the Upper Pigeon and the Lower Pigeon. Each section offers a different experience, making it ideal for a wide range of rafters—from families with young kids to thrill-seekers.

- **Upper Pigeon River:** The Upper Pigeon River offers Class III and IV rapids, which provide plenty of excitement for adventure lovers. Guided rafting tours last about 1.5 to 2 hours and cover approximately 5 miles of river, with several challenging rapids along the way. This section is best for those seeking a thrilling ride, though beginners are also welcome as experienced guides lead each trip. Expect to pay around $45-$55 per person for a standard guided trip.

Lower Pigeon River: The Lower Pigeon River is much calmer, featuring Class I and II rapids, making it perfect for families with children or those who prefer a more relaxed rafting experience. These trips are also 1.5 to 2 hours long, and the gentle ride gives you a chance to enjoy the scenic beauty of the river and surrounding forests. The cost for the Lower Pigeon experience typically ranges from $35-$45 per person.

Popular companies offering guided rafting trips include Smoky Mountain Outdoors, Rafting in the Smokies, and Wildwater Rafting. Most outfitters provide all the necessary gear, including helmets, life jackets, and paddles, and they give safety instructions before heading out on the river. Reservations are highly recommended, especially during peak summer months, and you can book your trip on the company websites, such as [Smoky Mountain

Outdoors](https://www.smokymountainrafting.com)
.

Ziplining in Gatlinburg

For a different kind of adventure that lets you take in the breathtaking views from above, ziplining in Gatlinburg is a must-try experience. There are several companies in the area that offer thrilling zipline courses that take you soaring above the treetops, providing a bird's-eye view of the Smokies.

Top Zipline Adventures

- **CLIMB Works Smoky Mountains:** Located just 10 minutes from downtown Gatlinburg, CLIMB Works is a well-known adventure company offering two zipline tours: Mountaintop Zipline Tour and Treetop Zipline Tour. The Mountaintop Tour features nine ziplines and offers expansive views of the Smoky Mountains, while the Treetop Tour takes you deeper into the lush forest canopy with nine ziplines, three sky bridges, and an ATV ride to the starting point. Prices start at $99 per person, with discounts for groups and children. More details and booking options are available at [CLIMB

Works Smoky Mountains](https://www.climbworks.com/smoky_mountains).

Legacy Mountain Ziplines: Just a short drive from Gatlinburg, Legacy Mountain Ziplines offers a zipline adventure that features seven zip lines stretching across 4.5 miles of cable, reaching heights of up to 500 feet. As you glide through the air, you'll enjoy sweeping views of the mountains and valleys below. The tour takes about 2.5 hours to complete and costs around $90 per person.

- **Gatlinburg Ziplines:** If you're looking for an option closer to downtown Gatlinburg, Gatlinburg Ziplines offers a more convenient experience. Their course features nine ziplines and is located just a few blocks from the Parkway, making it easy to fit into your itinerary. Prices start at $59 per person, and children as young as five can participate, making this a great choice for families.

What to Expect and Tips for Safety

- **Gear and Safety:** All zipline companies provide the necessary safety gear, including harnesses, helmets, and gloves, as well as professional guides who will help you every step of the way. A safety briefing is always given before you start, ensuring you understand the basics of braking, body positioning, and communication signals.

- **Dress Comfortably:** For both whitewater rafting and ziplining, it's essential to dress appropriately. Wear comfortable, moisture-wicking clothes and secure shoes. Sandals without straps or flip-flops are not recommended for either activity.
- **Weather Considerations:** Both activities are weather-dependent, and heavy rain or lightning may cause delays or cancellations. It's always a good idea to check the weather forecast before booking and to stay in touch with your tour operator for updates.

Cost and Booking Information

- **Whitewater Rafting:** Costs range from $35 to $55 per person, depending on the level of rapids and the type of experience you choose. Most companies offer discounts for larger groups.
- **Ziplining:** Costs typically range from $59 to $99 per person, depending on the location and length of the course. Discounts are often

available for families, groups, or if you book multiple activities.

Booking ahead is highly recommended, especially during summer when demand is at its peak. You can book directly through the companies' websites or by phone.

D. Camping in the Smokies

Frontcountry Campgrounds

For those who enjoy the comforts of a traditional campground with facilities, the Great Smoky Mountains National Park has ten frontcountry campgrounds that are perfect for families and casual campers. The frontcountry campgrounds are equipped with amenities like restrooms with flush toilets, drinking water, picnic tables, and fire rings. Below are some of the most popular campgrounds near Gatlinburg:

Elkmont Campground

Elkmont Campground is one of the largest and most popular campgrounds in the park, located just a short drive from downtown Gatlinburg. Nestled along the banks of the Little River, it offers easy access to popular hiking trails and scenic views, making it an excellent base camp for exploring the Smokies. Elkmont has 200 sites that can accommodate tents as well as RVs up to **32 feet. The cost to camp at Elkmont is approximately $30 per night.

- **Booking Information:** Reservations are required, especially during the peak season from April to October. You can make reservations through [Recreation.gov](https://www.recreation.gov).
- **Amenities:** The campground has flush toilets and potable water, but no showers or electric hookups.

Cades Cove Campground

Cades Cove Campground is another popular option, located in one of the park's most picturesque valleys. This campground gives you easy access to the Cades Cove Loop Road, where you can spot wildlife like black bears, white-tailed deer, and wild turkeys. The campground is open year-round, and sites cost around $25 per night. It's perfect for those who want to enjoy both camping and the scenic beauty of Cades Cove.

- **Booking Information:** Do the reservations by using the website above.
- **Amenities:** The campground includes potable water, flush toilets, and a camp store nearby, but does not have showers or electric hookups.

Backcountry Camping

For those who want to truly immerse themselves in nature, backcountry camping is the way to go. The Great Smoky Mountains National Park has over 100 backcountry campsites and shelters, which allow you to hike deep into the wilderness and enjoy the quiet beauty of the Smokies away from the crowds. Backcountry camping requires more preparation and a permit, which costs **$8 per person per night.

How to Get a Backcountry Permit

To camp in the backcountry, you must obtain a backcountry permit, which you can reserve and pay for online at [Recreation.gov](https://www.recreation.gov).
Make sure to plan your route and campsite well in advance, as some popular backcountry sites can fill up quickly. It's important to bring all the essentials,

including a map, compass, and enough food and water, as amenities are not available in the backcountry.

Group Camping

If you're traveling with a large group, the Smokies also offer group camping sites that can accommodate more than 20 people. These sites are perfect for scout troops, family reunions, or groups of friends looking for a shared outdoor adventure. Group sites are available at campgrounds such as Big Creek and Cataloochee, with costs ranging from $40 to $75 per night, depending on the size of the group. Reservations for group camping must be made in advance through [Recreation.gov](https://www.recreation.gov).

What to Expect During Your Stay

Camping in the Smokies offers a chance to unwind and reconnect with nature, but it also requires preparation to ensure a safe and enjoyable experience. Here are some key points to keep in mind:

- **Wildlife Safety:** The Smokies are home to a diverse range of wildlife, including black bears. Make sure to store all food and scented items in bear-proof containers or hang them at least 10 feet off the ground. Many campgrounds provide bear-proof lockers for food storage.

- **Campfires:** Campfires are allowed in designated fire rings only. Firewood can be purchased at the campgrounds, but it is illegal to bring your own firewood into the park to prevent the spread of pests.
- **Pack In, Pack Out:** All campers are required to leave no trace. This means packing out all trash and minimizing your impact on the environment.

What to Bring

- **Tent and Sleeping Gear:** Make sure to bring a tent, sleeping bags appropriate for the season, and sleeping pads for added comfort.
- **Cooking Supplies:** If you're staying at a frontcountry site, bring a camp stove or plan to cook over the fire ring. Don't forget essentials like a lighter, cookware, and food storage containers.
- **Clothing:** The weather in the Smokies can be unpredictable. Bring layers, as temperatures can vary significantly, especially in the spring and fall.

- **Essentials:** Flashlights, extra batteries, a first aid kit, and plenty of water or a water purification method are must-haves.

Best Time to Camp

The best time to camp in the Smokies depends on your personal preferences:

- Spring offers blooming wildflowers, but the weather can be wet, so prepare for rain.
- Summer is perfect for families, with warm temperatures and lots of activities, but campgrounds can be crowded.
- Fall is arguably the most beautiful time to visit, with the changing leaves creating a spectacular display of color.
- Winter offers solitude, but some campgrounds close, and temperatures can be chilly, so it's best for those experienced in cold-weather camping.

Chapter 6: Family-Friendly Activities

A. Best Attractions for Kids and Families

1. Ripley's Aquarium of the Smokies

Located right on the Parkway in downtown Gatlinburg, Ripley's Aquarium of the Smokies is an immersive experience where kids can explore and learn about marine life from around the world. This two-story aquarium consistently ranks among the top aquariums in the United States, and it offers a variety of interactive exhibits.

Location: 88 River Road, Gatlinburg, TN 37738. It's centrally located, and if you're staying in downtown Gatlinburg, it's within walking distance.

How to Get There: You can easily reach the aquarium on foot if you are staying downtown. Alternatively, the Gatlinburg Trolley has stops along the Parkway that can drop you close to the aquarium. For those driving in, parking is available nearby for around $10.

Highlights:

- **Shark Lagoon:** Kids will be thrilled to walk through the underwater tunnel where sharks and rays swim above and around them.
- **Penguin Playhouse:** The Penguin Playhouse offers a fun viewing experience with bubbles for kids to crawl into and get an up-close view of the penguins.
- **Touch-A-Ray Bay:** Kids can gently touch stingrays and learn about marine life in a safe environment.

Cost: $39.99 for adults and $24.99 for children (ages 6-11). Children under 5 are free. Purchase tickets in advance to save time: [Ripley's Aquarium Gatlinburg](https://www.ripleyaquariums.com/gatlinburg/).

Hours: Open daily from 9 a.m. to 10 p.m. during peak season.

2. Ober Gatlinburg Amusement Park & Ski Resort

Ober Gatlinburg is a unique mix of winter wonderland and amusement park. It's a great spot for family fun, whether you're visiting during the snowy winter months or sunny summer days.

Location: 1001 Parkway Suite 2, Gatlinburg, TN 37738.

How to Get There: You can take the Aerial Tramway from downtown Gatlinburg directly to the top of Ober Gatlinburg. The tram departs from 1001 Parkway and offers breathtaking views of the Smoky Mountains during the 10-minute ride. Tickets for the tram cost $19 for adults and $15 for children (ages 5-11). Alternatively, you can drive up the mountain to Ober Gatlinburg, with parking available for $10 per vehicle.

Highlights:

- **Ice Skating:** Enjoy year-round indoor ice skating at the Ober Gatlinburg ice rink—perfect for all ages.
- **Alpine Slide:** Glide down the mountainside on the Alpine Slide, a fun activity that allows parents and kids to control their speed.

- **Wildlife Encounter:** Kids will enjoy seeing black bears, river otters, and other native animals at the on-site wildlife encounter.

Cost: Entry to the park is free, but activities such as ice skating (around $12 per person) and Alpine Slide rides (approximately $8 per ride) have separate fees. For more details or to book tickets, visit [Ober Gatlinburg](https://obergatlinburg.com).

Hours: Open daily, hours vary based on season.

3. Anakeesta

Anakeesta is an outdoor family adventure park perched atop a mountain, blending natural beauty with fun activities for kids. It's one of Gatlinburg's newest and most exciting attractions for families.

Location: 576 Parkway, Gatlinburg, TN 37738.

How to Get There: To reach Anakeesta, you can choose to ride the Chondola (a chairlift and gondola combo) or the Ridge Rambler truck that takes you up to the summit. The base station is conveniently located on the Parkway in downtown Gatlinburg.

Highlights:

- **Treehouse Village Adventure:** Kids can run, climb, and explore a series of interconnected treehouses and bridges.
- **Treetop Skywalk:** The Treetop Skywalk is the longest tree-based bridge walk in North America, giving families a unique view of the forest canopy.
- **Rail Runner Mountain Coaster:** The Rail Runner lets you and your kids control your speed as you descend the mountain on a single-rail coaster.

Cost: $36.99 for adults and $23.99 for children (ages 4-11), which includes the ride up the mountain and access to most attractions. Extra fees apply for activities like the zipline and Rail Runner. Tickets and details are available at [Anakeesta](https://www.anakeesta.com).

Hours: Open daily, generally from 10 a.m. to 8 p.m., though seasonal changes may occur.

4. Gatlinburg SkyLift Park

For stunning views and a bit of thrill, Gatlinburg SkyLift Park is a great family-friendly destination. The SkyLift takes you up Crockett Mountain, and from there, you have plenty to explore.

Location: 765 Parkway, Gatlinburg, TN 37738.

How to Get There: SkyLift Park is right on the Parkway in downtown Gatlinburg, making it very accessible by foot if you're staying nearby. You can also use the Gatlinburg Trolley or park in a nearby lot.

Highlights:

- **SkyBridge:** Walk across the SkyBridge, the longest pedestrian suspension bridge in North America, which features glass panels in the middle for a heart-pounding view below.
- **SkyTrail:** For families that enjoy light hiking, the SkyTrail offers an easy, scenic walk with viewing platforms and interactive exhibits along the way.
- **SkyDeck:** Relax on the SkyDeck and enjoy panoramic views of Gatlinburg and the Smokies.

Cost: Tickets are $34.95 for adults and $20.95 for children (ages 4-11). You can buy tickets at [Gatlinburg SkyLift Park](https://www.gatlinburgskylift.com).

Hours: Open daily, typically from 9 a.m. to 10 p.m., depending on the season.

5. Hillbilly Golf

Hillbilly Golf is Gatlinburg's most unique miniature golf experience, offering a quirky take on classic mini-golf with an Appalachian twist. The course is located on the side of a mountain, with holes set among old mining equipment, outhouses, and moonshine stills, giving it a distinctive hillbilly feel.

Location: 340 Parkway, Gatlinburg, TN 37738.

How to Get There: Hillbilly Golf is located right on the Parkway, and the best way to reach it is by walking if you're staying downtown. You can also drive and park nearby or use the Gatlinburg Trolley.

Highlights:

- **Mountain-Top Experience:** The adventure starts with a tram ride to the top of the mountain, from which you then putt your way back down.
- **Two 18-Hole Courses:** The courses feature a variety of quirky obstacles and fun surprises that make it enjoyable for all ages.

Cost: $13 for adults and $9 for children (ages 4-12). Open seasonally from April through November.

More details can be found at the course or by calling in advance.

Hours: Usually open from 10 a.m. to 10 p.m. during the season.

B. Interactive Museums and Fun Zones

For families visiting Gatlinburg, there's no shortage of fun, educational, and interactive attractions designed to entertain children and adults alike. Below, we'll guide you through the top family-friendly interactive museums and fun zones, along with information on costs, locations, and how to reach them.

1. Ripley's Believe It or Not! Odditorium

Ripley's Believe It or Not! Odditorium is a must-see attraction for families looking for a fun and quirky experience. It's a museum unlike any other, featuring a bizarre collection of oddities from around the world.

Location: 800 Parkway, Gatlinburg, TN 37738.

How to Get There: The Odditorium is located right on the Parkway in downtown Gatlinburg, making it easy to reach on foot if you're staying nearby. If driving, public parking is available along the

Parkway, usually for about $10 per vehicle. Alternatively, the Gatlinburg Trolley also stops near the Odditorium.

Highlights:

- **Interactive Exhibits:** Kids and adults can explore three floors of quirky, interactive exhibits featuring artifacts like shrunken heads, bizarre artworks, and unique human feats. The museum is both entertaining and educational, giving you insight into some of the world's most peculiar curiosities.
- **Hands-On Activities:** Interactive activities such as optical illusions and puzzles help engage kids and make the experience more immersive.

Cost: $24.99 for adults and $14.99 for children (ages 3-11). Tickets are available at the museum or online at [Ripley's Believe It or Not! Gatlinburg](https://www.ripleys.com/gatlinburg/odditorium/).

Hours: Open daily from 9 a.m. to 11 p.m., making it convenient to fit into your schedule after a day of exploring Gatlinburg.

2. Ripley's Super Fun Zone

For a lively experience the entire family can enjoy, Ripley's Super Fun Zone is an arcade packed with interactive games that both children and adults will enjoy. Whether you're in the mood for classic arcade games, redemption games, or family-friendly competitions, this fun zone has it all.

Location: 542 Parkway, Gatlinburg, TN 37738.

How to Get There: Ripley's Super Fun Zone is centrally located on the Parkway, right in the heart of downtown Gatlinburg. You can walk to it easily if you're already downtown or take the Gatlinburg Trolley to one of the nearby stops.

Highlights:

- **Arcade Games:** With everything from skeeball to air hockey, Ripley's Super Fun Zone is a great spot for families to bond and enjoy some friendly competition. Earn tickets as you play and redeem them for fun prizes!
- **Laser Tag:** A laser tag arena offers a chance for some action-packed fun. Families can team up or compete against each other in a safe, exciting environment.

Cost: Admission is free, but games and attractions operate on a pay-per-play basis. It's advisable to set aside $10-$20 per person for arcade games and laser tag for a couple of hours of fun.

Hours: Typically open daily from 10 a.m. to midnight, providing plenty of time for some late-night entertainment.

3. Ripley's Marvelous Mirror Maze

Ripley's Marvelous Mirror Maze offers a fun and slightly challenging experience as families work their way through a labyrinth of mirrors and lights. It's a great activity for kids and adults alike and an ideal way to enjoy a unique, laughter-filled adventure together.

Location: 623 Parkway, Gatlinburg, TN 37738.

How to Get There: Conveniently located on the Parkway, you can reach the Mirror Maze by walking from most downtown locations or hopping on the Gatlinburg Trolley.

Highlights:

- **Mirror Maze:** The maze is designed to test your sense of direction, with mirrored hallways and disorienting lights. It's an exciting adventure for kids who will enjoy the challenge of finding their way through.

- **Infinity Room:** The maze also includes an infinity room with lights that seem to stretch on forever, adding an extra element of excitement to the experience.

Cost: $12.99 per person, with combo tickets available if you plan on visiting other Ripley's attractions as well. Purchase tickets online at [Ripley's Marvelous Mirror Maze](https://www.ripleys.com/gatlinburg/mirror-maze/).

Hours: Open daily from 10 a.m. to 10 p.m., giving families plenty of flexibility to fit it into their day.

4. Gatlin's Fun Center

Gatlin's Fun Center offers a mix of indoor and outdoor activities that the entire family can enjoy. From mini-golf and bumper cars to escape games, there is no shortage of fun activities to choose from.

Location: 716 Parkway, Gatlinburg, TN 37738.

How to Get There: Located along the Parkway, Gatlin's Fun Center is easy to reach by foot or by using the Gatlinburg Trolley. Public parking is available nearby.

Highlights:

- **Mini-Golf:** Gatlin's features both indoor and outdoor mini-golf courses, with the indoor course offering a blacklight, space-themed experience. It's a fun way for families to spend an afternoon or evening.
- **Laser Tag:** The multi-level laser tag arena is perfect for kids looking to expend some energy in a friendly competition.
- **Escape Rooms:** Gatlin's also offers escape games that families can solve together—ideal for older kids who enjoy puzzles and mysteries.

Cost: Activities are priced separately, with mini-golf costing around $11.99 per person and laser tag costing approximately $9.99 per person. You can also buy combo packages to save money if you plan on doing multiple activities. Visit [Gatlin's Fun Center](https://www.gatlinsfuncenter.com) for details and booking.

Hours: Open daily from 10 a.m. to 11 p.m. during peak season.

5. Hollywood Star Cars Museum

The Hollywood Star Cars Museum is a great way for families to see some of the most famous cars from movies and TV shows. Featuring everything from the Batmobile to Back to the Future's DeLorean, it's a hit with kids who love cars and parents who appreciate the nostalgia of famous film vehicles.

Location: 914 Parkway, Gatlinburg, TN 37738.

How to Get There: The museum is located on the Parkway, which makes it very accessible if you're staying in downtown Gatlinburg. It's also close to parking lots for those driving in and accessible by Gatlinburg Trolley.

Highlights:

- **Movie Cars:** See over 40 famous vehicles, including cars from movies like Ghostbusters, The Fast and the Furious, and TV shows like The Munsters.
- **Photo Opportunities:** Visitors have the chance to take photos with the cars, and sometimes you can even sit inside them for a fee.

Cost: $14.99 for adults and $8.99 for children (ages 6-12). Children under 6 are free, and there are discounts for seniors. Tickets can be purchased at the entrance or online at [Hollywood Star Cars Museum](https://www.starcarstn.com).

Hours: Open daily from 9 a.m. to 10 p.m..

C. Nature Walks and Educational Tours

Here are some of the top nature walks and educational experiences that are perfect for families in Gatlinburg.

1. Sugarlands Valley Nature Trail

The Sugarlands Valley Nature Trail is a beautiful and family-friendly walking path located near the Sugarlands Visitor Center, just minutes from downtown Gatlinburg. It is the only wheelchair-accessible trail in the park, making it perfect for families with strollers or those who want an easy, relaxed walk.

- **Location:** 1420 Fighting Creek Gap Road, Gatlinburg, TN 37738.

- **How to Get There:** The trailhead is located right at the Sugarlands Visitor Center, just a couple of miles from Gatlinburg along Newfound Gap Road (U.S. Highway 441). You can drive to the visitor center, which offers free parking.

Highlights:

- **Easy Accessibility:** The trail is just 0.5 miles long and paved, making it ideal for young children and families looking for a gentle stroll.
- **Informational Signage:** Along the trail, you'll find interpretive signs that provide information about the park's plants, animals, and history. Kids will enjoy learning about the park's natural features while keeping an eye out for wildlife like squirrels, birds, and even deer.
- **River Views:** The trail runs alongside the West Prong of the Little Pigeon River, offering lovely views of the river and a great spot for a family photo.

Cost: Free of charge. No reservations are required, and the trail is accessible all year round.

Hours: Open daily from sunrise to sunset.

2. Junior Ranger Program at Great Smoky Mountains National Park

The Junior Ranger Program is an excellent way for kids to learn about the Smokies while having fun. Offered by the National Park Service, this program allows children to engage in interactive activities that teach them about the park's ecology, history, and conservation efforts.

How to Participate:

- Families can pick up a Junior Ranger Activity Booklet at any visitor center, including the Sugarlands Visitor Center or the Cades Cove Visitor Center.
- Children complete activities in the booklet, which can include nature walks, scavenger hunts, and learning about local wildlife.
- Once the activities are complete, children can return to a visitor center to receive an official Junior Ranger badge as a keepsake for their accomplishment.

Cost: The Junior Ranger booklet is available for a nominal fee of $3, making it a budget-friendly activity.

Hours: The program is self-guided and can be completed anytime during daylight hours. Visitor centers are open daily from 9 a.m. to 5 p.m..

3. Guided Ranger-Led Walks

The Great Smoky Mountains National Park offers ranger-led programs throughout the year, and these are fantastic opportunities for families to learn about the park from knowledgeable guides. Programs typically include guided nature walks, storytelling, and interactive presentations. Many of these programs are tailored specifically for children, making them ideal for family participation.

Location: Locations for ranger-led walks vary and include popular spots like the Sugarlands Visitor Center, Clingmans Dome, and Cades Cove.

How to Get There: The walks often start from key visitor centers or trailheads that are easily accessible by car. Parking is generally available nearby.

Highlights:

- **Educational Experiences:** Rangers provide insights into the park's history, plant life, and wildlife. They may also share traditional Appalachian stories and information about the area's human history.
- **Wildlife Viewing:** Some walks focus on wildlife observation, giving families a chance to see black bears, deer, and various bird species in their natural habitats.

Cost: Most ranger-led programs are free. However, it is recommended to check with the visitor center for schedules and any fees that may apply to specific tours.

Hours: Programs are usually scheduled during the spring, summer, and fall. Visit the Sugarlands Visitor Center or check the [Great Smoky Mountains National Park events page](https://www.nps.gov/grsm/planyourvisit/calendar.htm) for up-to-date schedules.

4. Roaring Fork Motor Nature Trail and Self-Guided Tours

The Roaring Fork Motor Nature Trail is a 5.5-mile one-way loop that offers a beautiful drive and several opportunities to stop and take short nature walks along the way. Families can enjoy exploring old cabins, seeing cascading streams, and learning about the early settlers in the area. Several self-guided walking paths along the trail provide educational experiences for the whole family.

Location: Access to the Roaring Fork Motor Nature Trail is from Historic Nature Trail Road, right near downtown Gatlinburg.

How to Get There: Drive along Historic Nature Trail Road to reach the entrance. The motor trail is one-way, so make sure to start at the correct point.

Highlights:

- **Nature Walks:** Short trails like Trillium Gap Trail (which leads to Grotto Falls) are perfect for families. Grotto Falls is a unique waterfall you can walk behind, which adds an element of adventure for kids.
- **Historic Cabins:** The route includes stops at old cabins, providing a glimpse into the lives of early Appalachian settlers.

Cost: The motor trail is free to enter, but you will need a $5 parking tag if you plan to park for longer than 15 minutes at any of the pull-offs.

Hours: The trail is open seasonally, typically from mid-March through November, and is open from sunrise to sunset.

5. Greenbrier Picnic Area and Porters Creek Trail

For a relaxed combination of picnicking and an easy nature walk, the Greenbrier Picnic Area is a great choice. It's a quiet and less-crowded area of the park, perfect for families looking to enjoy a day surrounded by nature. After a picnic, you can explore the Porters Creek Trail, an easy trail that winds through the forest, featuring old homesteads and beautiful wildflowers in the spring.

Location: Greenbrier Road, approximately 6 miles east of Gatlinburg.

How to Get There: From Gatlinburg, take Highway 321 east for about 6 miles before turning onto Greenbrier Road. Follow it to the Greenbrier Picnic Area, where parking is available.

Highlights:

- **Family Picnic:** Set up a picnic alongside the Little Pigeon River and enjoy the peaceful sound of the water while surrounded by beautiful forest scenery.
- **Porters Creek Trail:** This trail is 4 miles round-trip and relatively easy, making it suitable for families. It offers great views of spring wildflowers, old stone walls, and remnants of historic settlements.

Cost: Free of charge. The parking tag of $5 per day is required for parking.

Hours: Open daily from sunrise to sunset.

Chapter 7: Gatlinburg's Culinary Scene

A. Best Restaurants and Local Eats

1. The Peddler Steakhouse

The Peddler Steakhouse is a long-time favorite in Gatlinburg, known for its mountain lodge atmosphere, stunning views of the Little Pigeon River, and top-quality steaks cooked to perfection. Located right at the entrance of the Great Smoky Mountains National Park, it has become a staple for visitors seeking a memorable dining experience.

Location: 820 River Road, Gatlinburg, TN 37738.

How to Get There: Located just off the Parkway, The Peddler is easy to reach from downtown

Gatlinburg. Parking is available at the restaurant, or you can take the Gatlinburg Trolley, which stops nearby.

Menu Highlights:

- **Hand-Cut Steaks:** The steaks are cut tableside, and you can choose the size that suits your appetite. The Ribeye and New York Strip are highly recommended.
- **Salad Bar:** The Peddler is famous for its extensive salad bar, featuring a variety of fresh vegetables, toppings, and house-made dressings.

Cost: Steaks start at around $30-$40, with additional sides and desserts available. While it's a bit pricier than other options in town, the quality of the food and the atmosphere make it worth it for a special night out.

Hours: Open daily for dinner from 5:00 p.m. to 9:30 p.m. Reservations are recommended, especially during peak tourist seasons. For more information, visit [The Peddler Steakhouse](https://peddlergatlinburg.com).

2. Pancake Pantry

A trip to Gatlinburg wouldn't be complete without breakfast at the Pancake Pantry. Established in 1960, it's Tennessee's first pancake house and has since become an iconic spot for tourists and locals alike. The menu boasts over 20 different types of pancakes, each one more delicious than the last.

Location: 628 Parkway, Gatlinburg, TN 37738.

How to Get There: Located directly on the Parkway, Pancake Pantry is easy to reach on foot from most downtown locations. There is also public parking nearby if you are driving.

Menu Highlights:

- **Sweet Potato Pancakes:** A local favorite, these pancakes are fluffy and perfectly seasoned, served with powdered sugar and cinnamon cream syrup.
- **Wild Blueberry Pancakes:** Made with fresh wild blueberries and served with whipped butter and blueberry compote, these are perfect for anyone who loves classic breakfast flavors.

Cost: Most pancake plates are priced between $10 and $15, making it an affordable and tasty breakfast option for the whole family.

Hours: Open daily from 7:00 a.m. to 3:00 p.m. It's a good idea to arrive early, as this popular spot often has a line out the door. For more details, visit [Pancake Pantry](https://www.pancakepantry.com).

3. Cherokee Grill

Cherokee Grill is another excellent choice for those looking for a slightly upscale dining experience in a casual yet refined atmosphere. Known for its mountain lodge decor, Cherokee Grill serves a mix of classic Southern dishes, fresh seafood, and expertly prepared steaks.

Location: 1002 Parkway, Gatlinburg, TN 37738.

How to Get There: The restaurant is conveniently located right along the Parkway, making it easy to reach on foot or by car. The Gatlinburg Trolley also stops nearby.

Menu Highlights:

- **Boursin Filet:** This is one of the most popular dishes on the menu—a tender filet topped with creamy boursin cheese and served with a side of mashed potatoes.
- **Shrimp & Grits:** A Southern classic made with sautéed shrimp, creamy grits, and a

flavorful sauce, perfect for those wanting to try regional cuisine.

Cost: Entrées are priced between $20 and $35, making Cherokee Grill a more moderately priced option for families and couples looking for a nice dinner.

Hours: Open daily from 4:00 p.m. to 10:00 p.m. Reservations are not required but recommended during busy periods.

4. Crockett's Breakfast Camp

For a hearty breakfast that will keep you fueled for a day of exploring the Smokies, Crockett's Breakfast Camp is a must-visit. The restaurant is themed after David "Crockett" Maples, a frontiersman who was known for feeding travelers hearty meals to keep them energized.

Location: 1103 Parkway, Gatlinburg, TN 37738.

How to Get There: Crockett's is located right along the Parkway, and it's an easy walk if you're staying downtown. Parking is available, and the Gatlinburg Trolley also has stops nearby.

Menu Highlights:

- **Black Bear Skillet:** Loaded with eggs, hash browns, sausage, bacon, ham, and cheese, this dish is perfect for those with a big appetite.
- **Aretha Frankenstein's Pancake Stack:** These oversized pancakes are fluffy, thick, and perfect for sharing. They are served with whipped butter and maple syrup, giving you a classic taste of the Smokies.

Cost: Most breakfast plates are priced between $10 and $18, and the portion sizes are generous, making it a good value for families.

Hours: Open daily from 7:00 a.m. to 1:00 p.m.

5. Calhoun's Gatlinburg

Calhoun's is a local chain that serves up delicious Southern BBQ and comfort food. Their Gatlinburg location features a warm, cozy atmosphere, perfect for a family dinner after a long day of sightseeing.

Location: 1004 Parkway, Gatlinburg, TN 37738.

How to Get There: Calhoun's is located on the Parkway and is easy to reach by foot or car, with public parking available nearby.

Menu Highlights:

- **Smoked Baby Back Ribs:** These tender ribs are slow-cooked and basted with Calhoun's signature BBQ sauce, served with sides like mac and cheese or coleslaw.
- **Ale Steak:** Marinated in their Cherokee Red Ale, this steak is cooked to your liking and is a favorite among locals and visitors.

Cost: Most entrées are between $15 and $25, making Calhoun's a budget-friendly option for a hearty and satisfying meal.

Hours: Open daily from 11:00 a.m. to 10:00 p.m.

B. Southern Cuisine Must-Try Dishes

1. Biscuits and Gravy

Biscuits and gravy is a Southern classic that you simply must try while visiting Gatlinburg. Soft, fluffy biscuits are served smothered in creamy sausage gravy, made from milk, flour, and plenty of crumbled breakfast sausage. It's a hearty and savory dish that's perfect for breakfast or brunch and is popular across many of Gatlinburg's restaurants.

Where to Try: Crockett's Breakfast Camp is known for serving some of the best biscuits and

gravy in town. Their freshly baked biscuits are topped with rich, flavorful sausage gravy that keeps guests coming back.
Cost: A plate of biscuits and gravy at Crockett's typically costs around $10 to $12, and the generous portion size makes it a great value.

Location: 1103 Parkway, Gatlinburg, TN 37738. Easily accessible from the Parkway, with parking available nearby.

Hours: Open daily from 7:00 a.m. to 1:00 p.m.

2. Fried Green Tomatoes

Another classic Southern dish is fried green tomatoes. Sliced unripe green tomatoes are coated in a seasoned cornmeal breading and then fried until they are crispy and golden. The dish has a slightly tart flavor that balances perfectly with the crunchy exterior, making it a popular starter or side.

Where to Try: Cherokee Grill serves a delicious version of fried green tomatoes as an appetizer, often paired with a remoulade dipping sauce that adds a touch of spice and tang.
Cost: The fried green tomatoes appetizer at Cherokee Grill costs around **$10**, making it an

affordable and tasty way to sample a Southern staple.

Location: 1002 Parkway, Gatlinburg, TN 37738. Located right on the Parkway, making it easy to access by foot or by car.

Hours: Open daily from 4:00 p.m. to 10:00 p.m.

3. Chicken and Dumplings

Chicken and dumplings is the ultimate comfort food—a hearty, warming dish featuring tender pieces of chicken simmered in a rich broth with fluffy dumplings. This traditional dish has been a favorite in Southern households for generations and is perfect for those cooler mountain evenings.

Where to Try: The Old Mill Restaurant, located in nearby Pigeon Forge, is well-known for its chicken and dumplings. The dish is served with a side of cornbread and Southern-style green beans, giving you the full Southern experience.
Cost: A plate of chicken and dumplings at The Old Mill costs approximately $18, and the meal comes with several side dishes, making it a great value for those who love hearty, home-cooked flavors.

Location: 164 Old Mill Ave, Pigeon Forge, TN 37863. It's a short drive from Gatlinburg, making it an easy addition to your trip if you want to try some of the best Southern comfort food in the area.

Hours: Open daily from 11:00 a.m. to 9:00 p.m.

4. BBQ Pulled Pork

Pulled pork is a quintessential dish of the South, and Gatlinburg has plenty of places that serve it with their own unique twist. Pulled pork is slow-cooked for hours until it's tender enough to be "pulled" apart, then coated with smoky, sweet, or spicy barbecue sauce.

Where to Try: Calhoun's is a local favorite for BBQ, and their pulled pork is particularly popular. It's served with a choice of sides, including mac and cheese, coleslaw, and hushpuppies.
Cost: A pulled pork plate at Calhoun's is priced around $15-$18, depending on the side dishes chosen. The hearty portions make it a fantastic choice for those who want a true taste of Tennessee barbecue.

Location: 1004 Parkway, Gatlinburg, TN 37738. Located right along the Parkway, accessible on foot or by car.

Hours: Open daily from 11:00 a.m. to 10:00 p.m.

5. Catfish

Fried catfish is a beloved Southern specialty that is crispy on the outside and tender on the inside. It's usually coated in a cornmeal batter and fried until golden brown, served with a side of tartar sauce, hushpuppies, and coleslaw.

Where to Try: Smoky Mountain Trout House offers a variety of fish dishes, including Southern-fried catfish. The catfish is caught fresh and prepared with a traditional cornmeal breading that gives it that authentic Southern flavor.
Cost: A fried catfish dinner at Smoky Mountain Trout House typically costs around $20, and it comes with sides like hushpuppies, which makes it a filling and satisfying meal.

Location: 410 Parkway, Gatlinburg, TN 37738. Conveniently located right off the Parkway, with easy access from downtown Gatlinburg.

Hours: Open daily from 4:00 p.m. to 9:00 p.m.

6. Country Ham and Red-Eye Gravy

Country ham with red-eye gravy is a traditional Appalachian dish that's salty, smoky, and utterly satisfying. The red-eye gravy is made using the drippings from the fried ham, with a splash of black coffee, creating a thin, flavorful sauce that is unique to Southern cooking.

Where to Try: The Applewood Farmhouse Restaurant in Sevierville, a short drive from Gatlinburg, serves an excellent version of this dish. The ham is paired with fluffy biscuits and sides like grits or fried apples for a complete Southern breakfast or lunch.
Cost: The cost for a plate of country ham with red-eye gravy is around $15, and the meal comes with a range of traditional side dishes, giving you a full taste of Appalachian flavors.

Location: 240 Apple Valley Road, Sevierville, TN 37862. The restaurant is located in Apple Barn Village, about a 20-minute drive from Gatlinburg.

Hours: Open daily from 8:00 a.m. to 9:00 p.m.

C. Cafes, Breweries, and Wineries

1. The Village Café & Creamery

Nestled in the charming atmosphere of The Village Shops, The Village Café & Creamery offers a cozy setting perfect for a coffee break or a sweet treat. The café is surrounded by cobblestone pathways and quaint storefronts, making it a picturesque spot for families and couples alike.

Location: 634 Parkway #4, Gatlinburg, TN 37738.

How to Get There: Located in the heart of The Village Shops, it's easily accessible from the Parkway by walking. Parking is available in the public lots along the Parkway.

Menu Highlights:

- **Espresso Drinks:** They serve a variety of coffee drinks, from lattes to cappuccinos, crafted using high-quality beans and fresh milk.
- **Ice Cream and Treats:** The café also offers a selection of hand-scooped ice cream, perfect for cooling down after a hot day of exploring. Their waffle cones are freshly made in-house, adding to the experience.

Cost: Coffee drinks range from $3 to $6, while ice cream is priced at $4 to $8 depending on the size and number of scoops.

Hours: Open daily from 10:00 a.m. to 9:00 p.m..

2. Gatlinburg Brewing Company

For craft beer lovers, the Gatlinburg Brewing Company is a must-visit. Known for its locally brewed beers, it's a popular spot for those who want to relax and unwind with friends or family after a day of hiking or sightseeing. They offer a wide selection of beer styles, from IPAs to stouts, each brewed on-site using locally sourced ingredients.

Location: 458 Parkway, Gatlinburg, TN 37738.

How to Get There: Situated right on the Parkway, the Gatlinburg Brewing Company is easy to find, with public parking nearby. You can also reach it using the Gatlinburg Trolley.

Menu Highlights:

- **Craft Beer:** Popular beers include the Space Needle IPA, a hoppy and refreshing brew, and the Roaring Fork Blonde, which is light and perfect for casual sipping.
- **Food Options:** In addition to beer, the brewery serves wood-fired pizzas, including options like the Margherita and the Smoky Mountain BBQ Pizza.

Cost: A pint of beer is priced between $6 and $8, and pizzas range from $12 to $18.

Hours: Open daily from 11:00 a.m. to 11:00 p.m..

3. Coffee & Company

Located in the picturesque Village Shops, Coffee & Company is a charming local café offering some of the best coffee in Gatlinburg. It's an ideal stop for those looking for a relaxing environment to enjoy a cup of freshly brewed coffee or a homemade pastry.

Location: 634 Parkway #13, Gatlinburg, TN 37738.

How to Get There: The café is located within The Village Shops, right off the Parkway. It's a short walk from most downtown hotels, and there are public parking options nearby.

Menu Highlights:

- **Locally Roasted Coffee:** Coffee & Company serves locally roasted coffee, ensuring a fresh and authentic flavour. Their specialty lattes are a popular choice, with flavors like Hazelnut Truffle and Caramel Macchiato.

Pastries and Sweets: They offer a selection of freshly baked pastries, muffins, and cookies, making it an ideal spot for a morning coffee or afternoon snack.

Cost: Coffee drinks range from $3 to $5, and pastries are priced at around $3 to $4 each.

Hours: Open daily from 8:30 a.m. to 6:00 p.m.. For more information, visit [Coffee & Company](https://thevillageshops.com).

4. Sugarland Cellars Winery

Sugarland Cellars is a local winery offering free wine tastings and tours, allowing visitors to sample a range of wines made from locally grown grapes. The winery captures the spirit of the Smokies with wines that are named after local landmarks and have flavours inspired by the region.

Location: 1133 Parkway, Gatlinburg, TN 37738.

How to Get There: Located right on the Parkway at the entrance to the Great Smoky Mountains National Park, Sugarland Cellars is easy to find and offers parking for visitors.

Menu Highlights:

- **Wine Selection:** Some of their bestsellers include the Hellbender Red, a semi-sweet red wine, and the Elkmont, a crisp, dry white wine. Each bottle tells a story of the Smokies, making it a great souvenir.
- **Free Tastings:** Sugarland Cellars offers free wine tastings every day, allowing visitors to try different varieties before making a purchase.

Cost: Wine tastings are free, and bottles of wine are available for purchase, ranging from $15 to $30.

Hours: Open daily from 10:00 a.m. to 7:00 p.m..

5. Tennessee Homemade Wines

Tennessee Homemade Wines is another fantastic spot to sample the local flavours of the Smokies. They specialize in traditional Southern sweet wines, crafted using locally grown fruits. It's an enjoyable experience for anyone who appreciates wine or wants to try something unique to the region.

Location: 643 Parkway, Gatlinburg, TN 37738.

How to Get There: Tennessee Homemade Wines is located on the Parkway, making it an easy stop as you explore downtown Gatlinburg.

Menu Highlights:

- **Sweet Wines:** Known for their Southern-style sweet wines, popular varieties include the Blackberry Wine and Blueberry Bammer. These wines are rich, fruity, and perfectly suited for those who enjoy a sweeter flavour profile.
- **Free Tastings:** Free tastings are available daily, and the knowledgeable staff is more than happy to help you find a wine that suits your taste.

Cost: Tastings are free, and bottles of wine are priced between $15 and $25.

Hours: Open daily from 10:00 a.m. to 11:00 p.m..

Chapter 8: Shopping in Gatlinburg

A. Best Souvenir Shops and Local Crafts

1. The Village Shops

The Village Shops is a collection of boutique stores that have a quaint European village charm. Located in downtown Gatlinburg, this shopping area is known for its unique specialty shops that offer a wide variety of souvenirs, crafts, and gifts. The cobblestone paths and old-world architecture make shopping here a truly enjoyable experience.

Location: 634 Parkway, Gatlinburg, TN 37738.

How to Get There: Located directly along the Parkway, The Village Shops are easy to access by foot. There is also public parking** available nearby.

Shops to Visit:

- **The Day Hiker:** A great place for outdoor enthusiasts, this shop offers hiking gear, maps, books, and Smoky Mountains-themed souvenirs such as T-shirts, mugs, and patches.
- **The Honey Pot:** If you're looking for locally crafted gifts, The Honey Pot has a wide selection of pottery, candles, and charming kitchen items—all made in Tennessee.

Hours: Shops are generally open daily from 10:00 a.m. to 6:00 p.m., though individual store hours may vary. Visit [The Village Shops](https://thevillageshops.com) for more information.

2. NOC Gatlinburg (Nantahala Outdoor Center)

For those who love outdoor adventure, the Nantahala Outdoor Center (NOC) offers more than just rafting and gear rentals. NOC Gatlinburg features an outdoor-focused souvenir shop that offers branded gear, Smoky Mountains apparel, and nature-themed gifts.

Location: 1138 Parkway, Gatlinburg, TN 37738.

How to Get There: Located near the downtown area, NOC is easily accessible on foot or by car, with public parking nearby.

What to Buy:

- **Outdoor Gear:** Branded merchandise like NOC T-shirts, hiking accessories, and trail guides make excellent gifts for adventure enthusiasts.
- **Unique Souvenirs:** The store also sells items like campfire mugs and ornaments, perfect for remembering your trip to the Smokies.

Cost: Prices vary based on the type of merchandise. T-shirts start at $20, while more specialized outdoor gear costs more depending on the product.

Hours: Open daily from 9:00 a.m. to 9:00 p.m..

3. Smoky Mountain Spinnery

If you're looking for a unique and local touch, Smoky Mountain Spinnery offers handmade fiber crafts, yarn, and a variety of locally sourced goods. This shop is perfect for those who are into knitting, crocheting, or simply want a cozy souvenir made from locally spun wool.

Location: 466 Brookside Village Way, Gatlinburg, TN 37738.

How to Get There: Smoky Mountain Spinnery is located just off the Parkway, near the heart of Gatlinburg. There is public parking available nearby.

What to Buy:

- **Hand-Dyed Yarns:** The shop offers an impressive selection of hand-dyed yarns, sourced from local farms in the region.
- **Knitted Items:** For those who don't knit themselves, there are hand-knitted scarves, hats, and mittens available, perfect for a unique, warm keepsake.

Cost: Yarn skeins start at $15, while hand-knitted items vary based on complexity, ranging from $20 to $50.

Hours: Open daily from 10:00 a.m. to 6:00 p.m.

4. Ole Smoky Candy Kitchen

For those with a sweet tooth, Ole Smoky Candy Kitchen is the perfect spot for edible souvenirs. This classic candy store has been making homemade sweets since 1950 and is known for its old-fashioned taffy, fudge, and chocolates.

Location: 744 Parkway, Gatlinburg, TN 37738.

How to Get There: Located right on the Parkway in downtown Gatlinburg, it's easily accessible by walking from most hotels and other attractions. Public parking is also available nearby.

What to Buy:

- **Taffy:** Watch taffy being made on-site and take home a box of assorted flavors for a fun, nostalgic treat.
- **Homemade Fudge:** Their rich fudge comes in a variety of flavors like chocolate walnut, maple, and peanut butter—perfect for sharing (or keeping all to yourself!).

Cost: Taffy is priced at $7.50 per box, and fudge starts at $8 per half-pound.

Hours: Open daily from 9:00 a.m. to 9:00 p.m.. For more information, visit [Ole Smoky Candy Kitchen](https://olesmokycandykitchen.com).

5. Gatlinburg SkyLift Park Gift Shop

Located at the top of Crockett Mountain, the Gatlinburg SkyLift Park Gift Shop offers stunning views along with a great selection of souvenirs that are specific to the Smoky Mountains. Whether you're looking for unique T-shirts, mugs, or keychains, this gift shop has plenty of options for you.

Location: 765 Parkway, Gatlinburg, TN 37738.

How to Get There: You can take the Gatlinburg SkyLift to reach the shop at the summit. The SkyLift entrance is located on the Parkway, and public parking is available nearby.

What to Buy:

- **Mountain-Themed Apparel:** Get a Gatlinburg SkyLift T-shirt or hoodie to commemorate your visit.
- **Local Souvenirs:** Items like magnets, keychains, and postcards featuring the Smoky Mountains make perfect gifts for friends and family.

Cost: T-shirts are priced around $20 to $25, and smaller souvenirs like magnets and keychains are available for $5 to $10.

Hours: Open daily, generally from 9:00 a.m. to 10:00 p.m. depending on the season.

B. Arts and Crafts Community in the Smokies

1. Great Smoky Arts & Crafts Community Loop

The Arts & Crafts Community Loop is an 8-mile circle of studios, galleries, and workshops that offers an immersive experience for those interested in Appalachian crafts. Here, you can find handmade pottery, beautiful wood carvings, intricate glasswork, and much more. Each artisan's studio offers something unique, and many artisans are happy to share stories about their work, techniques, and inspirations.

Location: The loop is located along Glades Road and Buckhorn Road, just a short drive from downtown Gatlinburg.

How to Get There: You can reach the Arts & Crafts Community Loop by driving about 3 miles east from downtown Gatlinburg along Highway 321, then turning onto Glades Road. There is also a Gatlinburg Trolley that serves the area, making it easy to explore without having to drive yourself.

Hours: Most of the shops and studios are open Monday through Saturday, typically from 10:00 a.m. to 5:00 p.m., but hours may vary, so it's always best to check with individual artisans if you have a specific studio in mind.

Highlights of the Community

Alewine Pottery: One of the most well-known shops in the Arts & Crafts Community, Alewine Pottery specializes in beautifully hand-thrown pottery that is both decorative and functional. Known for its nature-inspired glazes and leaf imprints, this family-owned studio has been creating stunning pottery for decades. Visitors can watch the pottery-making process while browsing the shop.

- **Cost:** Items range from $20 for small pieces to $200 for larger items.
- **Location:** 623 Glades Road, Gatlinburg, TN 37738.
- **Hours:** Open daily from 10:00 a.m. to 5:00 p.m.. More information is available at [Alewine Pottery](https://www.alewinepottery.net).

Cliff Dwellers Gallery: Originally established in 1933 in the Smokies, Cliff Dwellers Gallery is a cooperative showcasing the work of several artists, including painters, weavers, and jewelry makers. The gallery offers a wide selection of handcrafted items, ranging from intricate baskets to handwoven scarves and quilts. Visitors can learn about the local traditions behind each piece, making every item more meaningful.

- **Cost:** Prices vary, with smaller items like handmade candles starting at $15, and larger items like woven baskets ranging up to $200.
- **Location:** 668 Glades Road, Gatlinburg, TN 37738.
- **Hours:** Open from 10:00 a.m. to 5:00 p.m. daily.

Buie Pottery: Another notable shop in the Arts & Crafts Community is Buie Pottery, where you can find hand-thrown stoneware crafted with a unique approach to traditional pottery techniques. Each piece is made with a dedication to both form and function, resulting in beautiful mugs, plates, and bowls that are meant to be used and enjoyed.

- **Cost:** Items are generally priced from $25 for small mugs to $150 for more elaborate pieces.
- **Location:** 1360 East Parkway, Gatlinburg, TN 37738.
- **Hours:** Open Monday through Saturday from 10:00 a.m. to 5:00 p.m..

2. Hands-On Experiences and Workshops

One of the unique aspects of visiting the Arts & Crafts Community is the opportunity to engage with the artisans and even participate in workshops:

Great Smoky Arts & Crafts School: For those interested in learning more about Appalachian crafts, the Great Smoky Arts & Crafts School offers classes and workshops throughout the year. Learn how to make pottery, weave baskets, or create your own stained glass piece with instruction from local artisans.

- **Cost:** Classes typically range from $50 to $150, depending on the materials and duration.
- **Booking:** Advance booking is recommended, especially during peak seasons.

Fireside Weaving Studio: Another hands-on experience is offered by Fireside Weaving Studio, where you can learn the basics of weaving using traditional looms. You'll get to take home your woven creation, whether it's a simple coaster or a decorative wall hanging.

- **Cost:** Workshops are priced around $60, and all materials are provided.

Shopping Tips

- **Plan Your Visit:** The Arts & Crafts Community loop is extensive, so it's best to plan your visit ahead of time and decide which shops you want to see first. Maps of the community are available at most local visitor centers and online.
- **Bring Cash:** While many artisans accept credit cards, it's a good idea to bring some cash, especially if you plan to visit smaller workshops where only cash payments are accepted.
- **Talk to the Artists:** One of the most rewarding parts of visiting the Arts & Crafts Community is getting to know the artisans. Many of them love to share their techniques and the history behind their craft, which makes purchasing a handmade item even more special.

C. Where to Find Unique Handmade Items

Here are some of the best places to find unique handmade items during your visit.

1. Great Smoky Arts & Crafts Community

The Great Smoky Arts & Crafts Community is the perfect place to discover truly unique handmade items crafted by local artisans. As North America's largest group of independent artisans, this community is home to over 100 artists, each offering something distinct—whether it's pottery, wood carvings, or textiles. The 8-mile loop along Glades Road and Buckhorn Road features a collection of individual studios, galleries, and shops, all of which specialize in traditional and contemporary crafts.

Location: The community loop is located about 3 miles from downtown Gatlinburg, along Glades Road and Buckhorn Road.

How to Get There: You can drive directly to the community, or take the Gatlinburg Trolley, which provides convenient service to the area.

What to Find:

- **Handmade Pottery:** Shops like Alewine Pottery offer a wide selection of hand-thrown, nature-inspired pottery pieces—everything from mugs to dinnerware.
- **Wooden Carvings and Sculptures:** Ogle's Broom Shop is known for its intricately carved brooms, while other artisans in the

community specialize in wooden figurines, sculptures, and handcrafted furniture.

- **Handwoven Baskets:** Cliff Dwellers Gallery is a fantastic spot to find intricately woven baskets, which have been crafted using traditional Appalachian methods.

Hours: Most shops are open daily from 10:00 a.m. to 5:00 p.m., though individual shop hours may vary. For more information, visit [Great Smoky Arts & Crafts Community](https://www.gatlinburgcrafts.com).

2. Santa's Claus-et

Santa's Claus-et is one of Gatlinburg's hidden gems, featuring handmade Christmas ornaments, decorations, and gifts. This cozy shop is perfect for those who want to take home a bit of the holiday spirit all year long. Every item in the shop is handcrafted with care, and you can find a variety of unique Christmas-themed souvenirs.

Location: 1350 East Parkway, Gatlinburg, TN 37738.

How to Get There: Santa's Claus-et is located just off Highway 321, making it easy to reach by car. There is free parking available at the shop.

What to Find:

- **Handmade Ornaments:** The shop offers a variety of unique, handcrafted ornaments, many of which are made by local artisans and feature Smoky Mountain themes.
- **Holiday Decor:** Along with ornaments, you can also find handmade Christmas decor, including wreaths, stockings, and tree toppers.

Cost: Ornaments start at around $10, while more elaborate pieces like wreaths can cost up to $50 or more.

Hours: Open Monday through Saturday from 10:00 a.m. to 5:00 p.m..

3. Buie Pottery

Buie Pottery is a wonderful place to find handmade stoneware that has both a functional and artistic purpose. Each piece is crafted on-site by Brenda Buie, who uses her unique style to create beautiful glazes and designs that reflect the surrounding natural beauty of the Smoky Mountains. Items such as mugs, bowls, vases, and serving platters are available, and each piece is one-of-a-kind.

Location: 1360 East Parkway, Gatlinburg, TN 37738.

How to Get There: Located on the Arts & Crafts Loop, Buie Pottery is accessible by car, and parking is available nearby.

What to Find:

- **Functional Pottery:** Buie Pottery offers a selection of mugs, plates, and serving bowls, all of which are both beautiful and practical. Each piece features natural, earthy colors inspired by the Smoky Mountains.
- **Decorative Pieces:** In addition to functional pottery, you'll also find decorative vases and wall plaques that make great gifts or souvenirs.

Cost: Prices range from $20 for mugs to over $100 for more elaborate pieces like large serving platters.

Hours: Open Monday through Saturday from 10:00 a.m. to 5:00 p.m..

4. Firefly Glass Studio

Firefly Glass Studio is a great place to find colorful, handcrafted glass items. Local artisans craft each piece, offering a selection of decorative and functional glasswork. This studio is known for its stunning glass ornaments, suncatchers, and jewelry, each made using traditional glassblowing techniques.

Location: 600 Glades Road, Suite 3, Gatlinburg, TN 37738.

How to Get There: Located on Glades Road within the Arts & Crafts Community, Firefly Glass Studio is easily accessible by car, with plenty of parking nearby.

What to Find:

- **Glass Ornaments:** Beautiful, hand-blown glass ornaments are available in a variety of colors and designs—perfect for adding a touch of sparkle to your holiday decor or as a year-round decoration.
- **Jewelry:** Handmade glass pendants and earrings are available, each one unique due to the nature of the glassblowing process.

Cost: Ornaments start at $20, while jewelry pieces are typically priced between $25 and $50.

Hours: Open daily from 10:00 a.m. to 5:00 p.m..

5. Cliff Dwellers Gallery

Cliff Dwellers Gallery is a wonderful spot to find handmade items crafted by local artisans. This gallery features work from a variety of artists, including jewelry makers, painters, basket weavers, and fiber artists. It's the perfect place to find a wide selection of locally made crafts in one location.

Location: 668 Glades Road, Gatlinburg, TN 37738.

How to Get There: Located within the Arts & Crafts Community Loop on Glades Road, the gallery is easy to reach by car. There is plenty of free parking available.

What to Find:

- **Handmade Jewelry:** The gallery offers an impressive collection of handmade jewelry, including necklaces, bracelets, and earrings, crafted by local artisans.

Weavings and Textiles: You can also find handwoven scarves, quilts, and other textiles, each made with care by local weavers using traditional techniques.

Cost: Jewelry pieces start at $30, and larger items like woven textiles range from $50 to $200.

Hours: Open daily from 10:00 a.m. to 5:00 p.m..

Tips for Finding Unique Handmade Items

- **Engage with Artisans:** Many artisans love to share their stories and the inspiration behind their work. Don't hesitate to ask questions or learn more about the techniques they use—it adds a personal touch to the items you buy.
- **Plan Your Time:** The Arts & Crafts Loop is extensive, so plan enough time to explore at your own pace. If possible, spend a half or full day exploring the shops to make the most of your experience.
- **Bring Cash:** While most shops accept credit cards, it's always a good idea to carry some cash, especially for smaller items or to tip artisans for demonstrations.

Chapter 9: Best Itineraries for Every Traveler

A. 3-Day Adventure for First-Time Visitors

Day 1: Discover Downtown Gatlinburg and Sky-High Views

Morning: Arrival and Downtown Exploration

Breakfast at Pancake Pantry: Start your day with a hearty breakfast at the Pancake Pantry—a Gatlinburg staple since 1960. Enjoy sweet potato pancakes or blueberry-stuffed crepes that will fuel your day of adventure.

- **Location:** 628 Parkway, Gatlinburg, TN 37738.
- **Cost:** Expect to spend $10-$15 per person.

Explore The Village Shops: After breakfast, take a stroll through The Village Shops. This charming area with cobblestone walkways features unique boutiques where you can find handcrafted gifts and souvenirs.

Afternoon: SkyLift Park and Ober Gatlinburg

Gatlinburg SkyLift Park: Ride the SkyLift to the top of Crockett Mountain and experience breathtaking views of the Smoky Mountains. Take a walk across the SkyBridge—the longest pedestrian suspension bridge in North America—and don't forget to snap a few pictures from the SkyDeck.

- **Cost:** $34.95 for adults, $20.95 for children.
- **Hours:** Typically open from 9:00 a.m. to 10:00 p.m..

Lunch at Ober Gatlinburg: After your visit to SkyLift Park, head over to Ober Gatlinburg via the Aerial Tramway. Enjoy lunch at one of their onsite restaurants, such as the Seasons of Ober Restaurant, where you can find sandwiches, soups, and daily specials.

- **Cost:** Aerial Tramway ticket is $19 for adults, $15 for children.

Evening: Dinner and Nighttime Stroll

Dinner at The Peddler Steakhouse: End your first day with dinner at The Peddler Steakhouse—an iconic spot located along the Little Pigeon River. Choose from their hand-cut steaks or opt for fresh trout caught right in the Smokies.

- **Cost:** Steaks start at $30.

Explore the Parkway at Night: The Parkway comes alive at night with twinkling lights and the sounds of live music. Grab an ice cream from Mad Dog's Creamery as you wander and take in the lively atmosphere.

Day 2: Great Smoky Mountains Adventure

Morning: Explore the Great Smoky Mountains National Park

Sugarlands Visitor Center: Begin your day at the Sugarlands Visitor Center to pick up a park map and learn about the history and ecology of the Great Smoky Mountains National Park. From there, set off on a short nature walk.

- **Cost:** Free.

Hike to Laurel Falls: Take a 2.6-mile round-trip hike to Laurel Falls, one of the most popular and picturesque waterfalls in the park. The hike is relatively easy, making it accessible for most travelers. The falls are at their most beautiful early in the morning before the crowds arrive.

Afternoon: Picnic and Roaring Fork Motor Nature Trail

Picnic at Metcalf Bottoms: Pack a picnic lunch or stop at a local deli to gather provisions and head to Metcalf Bottoms for a peaceful picnic by the river.

Roaring Fork Motor Nature Trail: Spend your afternoon on the Roaring Fork Motor Nature Trail. This 5.5-mile one-way loop offers stunning views, historic cabins, and several places where you can get out and stretch your legs. Make sure to stop at Grotto Falls, where you can take a short hike to see one of the only waterfalls in the park that you can walk behind.

Evening: Dinner and Moonshine Tasting

Dinner at Calhoun's: Wrap up your day of adventure with a Southern BBQ dinner at Calhoun's in downtown Gatlinburg. Enjoy pulled pork, ribs, or smoked chicken, along with classic sides like coleslaw and cornbread.

- **Cost:** Most entrées range from $15 to $25.

Visit Ole Smoky Moonshine Distillery: After dinner, head to Ole Smoky Moonshine Distillery for a tasting of authentic Tennessee moonshine. This iconic spot offers a variety of flavors, from classic white lightning to sweet peach moonshine.

- **Cost:** Tasting fee is $5, which includes a souvenir shot glass.

Day 3: Outdoor Adventures and Relaxation

Morning: Anakeesta and Tree Canopy Walks

Anakeesta: Start your morning by taking the Chondola up to Anakeesta—a mountaintop theme park. Enjoy the spectacular views of the Smokies, stroll through the Vista Gardens, and let your inner adventurer out on the Treetop Skywalk, which features hanging bridges that take you through the canopy.

- **Cost:** Admission is $36.99 for adults, $23.99 for children (ages 4-11).

Treehouse Village Adventure: Let the kids explore Treehouse Village, an interactive area filled with bridges, climbing elements, and views of the mountains.

Afternoon: River Tubing and Relaxing Lunch

River Tubing with River Rat Tubing: Drive over to nearby Townsend for a fun afternoon of river tubing with River Rat Tubing. It's a leisurely way to enjoy the Smoky Mountains from the water, perfect for cooling off and enjoying some family fun.

- **Cost:** $20 per person, includes rental and transportation back to the starting point.

Lunch at Smoky Mountain Brewery: Return to Gatlinburg and enjoy a casual lunch at the Smoky Mountain Brewery. Try one of their in-house brews alongside a delicious burger or wood-fired pizza.

- **Cost:** Most dishes range from $10 to $18.

Evening: Relaxing and Evening Entertainment

Relax at Salt & Pepper Shaker Museum: Take it easy after tubing by visiting the quirky Salt &

Pepper Shaker Museum—one of the world's only museums dedicated to salt and pepper shakers. It's a fun, quick stop that will entertain both kids and adults.

- **Cost:** $3 per person, which can be applied toward any purchase in the gift shop.

Dinner at Cherokee Grill: Finish your Gatlinburg adventure with dinner at Cherokee Grill. Known for its mountain lodge atmosphere, enjoy local favorites like Boursin Filet or shrimp and grits for your final meal in Gatlinburg.

- **Cost:** Entrées are priced between $20 and $35.

B. 7-Day In-Depth Exploration of Gatlinburg and the Smokies

This itinerary is perfect for those who want to delve deeper into Gatlinburg's local culture, outdoor activities, and Appalachian charm.

Day 1: Welcome to Gatlinburg

Morning: Arrival and Getting Oriented

Check-In and Settle Down: Start by checking into your hotel, cabin, or chalet. Consider booking a stay in the Arts & Crafts Community for a true Appalachian experience. This area provides access to unique local shops and charming accommodations with scenic views.

Breakfast at Crockett's Breakfast Camp: Begin your trip with a hearty breakfast at Crockett's Breakfast Camp, where you can try the famous Black Bear Skillet to kick off your adventure.

- **Location:** 1103 Parkway, Gatlinburg, TN 37738.

Cost: Expect to spend $12-$18.

Afternoon: Downtown Exploration

Visit the Great Smoky Mountains Heritage Center: Explore the Great Smoky Mountains Heritage Center to learn about the rich cultural history of the region, from the Native Americans to the early settlers.

- **Cost:** Admission is around $10.

The Village Shops: Spend the rest of your afternoon wandering around The Village Shops, enjoying the atmosphere and exploring specialty stores that offer local crafts, handmade pottery, and more.

Evening: Dinner and Nightlife

Dinner at Cherokee Grill: Enjoy dinner at Cherokee Grill, where you can savor local flavors like Boursin Filet or Mountain Trout.

- **Cost:** Entrées range from $20 to $35.

Explore the Parkway at Night: End your day by strolling along the Parkway, taking in the lights and lively atmosphere, and perhaps indulging in a dessert from Mad Dog's Creamery.

Day 2: Great Smoky Mountains National Park

Morning: Sugarlands Visitor Center and Hiking

Sugarlands Visitor Center: Start your day at the Sugarlands Visitor Center to gather information on trails and learn more about the park's history and wildlife.

- **Cost:** Free.

Hike to Chimney Tops: Take on the challenging yet rewarding Chimney Tops Trail. The hike is around 4 miles round-trip and offers incredible views from the top, making it a perfect start to your Smoky Mountains adventure.

Afternoon: Newfound Gap and Clingmans Dome

Newfound Gap: Drive along Newfound Gap Road and stop at the Newfound Gap Overlook. The view from this elevation is one of the most picturesque in the Smokies.

Clingmans Dome: Head further up to Clingmans Dome, the highest point in the park. Hike the short trail to the observation tower for panoramic views of the Smokies.

- **Cost:** Free, but a $5 parking tag is required.

Evening: Dinner at Calhoun's

Dinner at Calhoun's: Enjoy a BBQ dinner at Calhoun's. Try their signature Baby Back Ribs or the Pulled Pork Platter.

- **Cost:** Prices range from $15 to $25.

Day 3: Arts & Crafts Community

Morning and Afternoon: Arts & Crafts Community Exploration

Great Smoky Arts & Crafts Community: Spend your day driving along the Arts & Crafts Loop. Visit Alewine Pottery, Cliff Dwellers Gallery, and other artisan studios to see demonstrations and purchase handmade souvenirs.

- **Cost:** Free to explore, with optional purchases.

Evening: Dinner and Live Music

Dinner at Wild Plum Tea Room: Dine at the Wild Plum Tea Room, a quaint restaurant inspired by Austrian-style tea houses, offering unique and seasonal dishes.

- **Cost:** $15-$25 per person.

Live Music at Ole Red: For a taste of local entertainment, head to Ole Red for live country music and a drink or two to end your evening.

Day 4: Outdoor Adventure Day

Morning: Rafting the Pigeon River

Whitewater Rafting: Drive to Hartford, TN (about 30 minutes from Gatlinburg) for a whitewater rafting adventure on the Upper Pigeon River. Enjoy thrilling Class III and IV rapids with experienced guides.

- **Cost:** $50 per person for a guided trip.

Afternoon: Ziplining at CLIMB Works

Ziplining Adventure: In the afternoon, visit CLIMB Works Smoky Mountains for an adrenaline-pumping zipline tour through the forest canopy.

- **Cost:** $99 per person.

Evening: Dinner and Relaxation

Dinner at The Park Grill: Finish your day with dinner at The Park Grill, where you can enjoy a cozy mountain lodge atmosphere and Southern-inspired dishes like grilled moonshine chicken.

- **Cost:** $20-$35 per entrée.

Day 5: Nature Walks and Cades Cove

Morning: Cades Cove Loop Road

Cades Cove Scenic Drive: Drive the Cades Cove Loop, an 11-mile one-way road that offers some of the best wildlife viewing opportunities in the

Smokies. Make sure to stop at some of the historic cabins and churches along the way.

Afternoon: Abrams Falls Hike

Hike to Abrams Falls: Take the 5-mile round-trip hike to Abrams Falls, which is a moderate hike with a rewarding waterfall at the end. It's a great way to experience the natural beauty of the cove.

Evening: Dinner at Mel's Classic Diner

Drive to Pigeon Forge: Head over to Pigeon Forge for dinner at Mel's Classic Diner. This retro-style diner offers burgers, milkshakes, and comfort food classics.

- **Cost:** $10-$20 per person.

Day 6: Family-Friendly Fun and Anakeesta

Morning: Visit Ripley's Aquarium of the Smokies

Ripley's Aquarium: Spend the morning exploring Ripley's Aquarium, which is filled with interactive exhibits, from Shark Lagoon to Penguin Playhouse.

- **Cost:** $39.99 for adults, $24.99 for children.

Afternoon: Anakeesta Adventure

Anakeesta: Take the Chondola up to Anakeesta for a day filled with adventure. Enjoy the Treetop

Skywalk, the Vista Gardens, and the Rail Runner Mountain Coaster.

- **Cost:** $36.99 for adults, $23.99 for children.

Evening: Dinner at The Greenbrier

The Greenbrier Restaurant: For a fine dining experience, enjoy dinner at The Greenbrier, an upscale steakhouse with an extensive menu that includes fresh seafood and premium cuts of steak.

- **Cost:** $40 and up** per entrée.

Day 7: Scenic Drive and Relaxation

Morning: Roaring Fork Motor Nature Trail

Roaring Fork: Drive the Roaring Fork Motor Nature Trail, stopping at historic cabins and scenic overlooks. Take a short hike to Grotto Falls and enjoy the peaceful surroundings.

- **Cost:** Free, but a $5 parking tag is required.

Afternoon: Relax at the Spa

Spa Treatment at Riverstone Resort: After a week of adventure, relax with a spa treatment at the Riverstone Resort & Spa. Choose from massages, facials, and other services designed to help you unwind.

Cost: Treatments start at $100.

Evening: Final Dinner and Farewell

Dinner at Smoky Mountain Brewery: Enjoy your final dinner at Smoky Mountain Brewery, savoring one of their house-made brews with a pizza or burger.

- **Cost:** $15-$25 per person.

C. Family-Friendly Itinerary for Outdoor Fun

This family-friendly itinerary is designed to give you the best balance of fun, adventure, and relaxation that the Smokies have to offer.

Day 1: Introduction to Gatlinburg and Outdoor Adventure

Morning: Arrival and Pancake Breakfast

Breakfast at Pancake Pantry: Start your adventure with a hearty breakfast at Pancake Pantry, a beloved local spot with a kid-friendly atmosphere and a variety of pancake flavors, from chocolate chip to blueberry.

- **Cost:** $10-$15 per person.

Walk Through The Village Shops: After breakfast, take a walk through The Village Shops and let the kids explore the unique stores, from candy shops to toy stores, set in a charming village atmosphere.

Afternoon: Ripley's Aquarium of the Smokies

Ripley's Aquarium: Spend the afternoon at Ripley's Aquarium of the Smokies, one of the most popular family attractions in Gatlinburg. The Shark Lagoon Tunnel and the Penguin Playhouse are must-see exhibits, and the Touch-A-Ray Bay will allow kids to have a hands-on encounter with stingrays.

- **Cost:** $39.99 for adults, $24.99 for children (ages 6-11).

Lunch at Bubba Gump Shrimp Co.: After the aquarium, enjoy a casual lunch at Bubba Gump Shrimp Co., which has a kid-friendly menu and a fun atmosphere.

- **Cost:** $10-$20 per person.

Evening: Anakeesta Adventure Park

Anakeesta: Head up to Anakeesta for an evening of mountaintop adventure. Ride the Chondola to the summit, explore the Treehouse Village Adventure, and take a leisurely walk along the Treetop Skywalk.

- **Cost:** $36.99 for adults, $23.99 for children (ages 4-11).

Dinner at Anakeesta: Enjoy dinner at the Cliff Top Grill & Bar, with beautiful views overlooking the Smoky Mountains.

Day 2: Explore Nature and Adventure Parks

Morning: Great Smoky Mountains National Park

Sugarlands Visitor Center: Start your day at the Sugarlands Visitor Center to get oriented with the national park. This is a great place for kids to learn about the park's wildlife and see some of the exhibits.

Hike to Laurel Falls: Embark on an easy-to-moderate hike to Laurel Falls. This 2.6-mile round-trip trail is one of the most accessible hikes in the park and offers beautiful views of a waterfall at the end. It's suitable for young children, and they'll love splashing around near the falls (with supervision, of course).

Afternoon: Ober Gatlinburg Amusement Park

Ober Gatlinburg: Take the Aerial Tramway up to Ober Gatlinburg Amusement Park. Spend the afternoon enjoying family-friendly rides, like the Alpine Slide, or take the kids ice skating at the year-round indoor ice rink.

Cost: $19 for the Aerial Tramway, plus additional fees for activities like ice skating ($12 per person).

Evening: Dinner and Mountain Coaster Fun

Dinner at The Park Grill: After a day of exploring, head to The Park Grill for a family-friendly dinner. Their menu includes plenty of options that both kids and adults will enjoy, like mac and cheese or BBQ ribs.

- **Cost:** $15-$30 per entrée.

Gatlinburg Mountain Coaster: If the kids still have energy, end the night with a thrilling ride on the Gatlinburg Mountain Coaster. This ride is exciting but family-friendly, and you control your speed, making it perfect for all ages.

- **Cost:** $16 for adults, $13 for children.

Day 3: Scenic Drives and Family Fun

Morning: Cades Cove Loop and Picnic

Cades Cove Scenic Drive: Drive through Cades Cove, an 11-mile loop road known for its beautiful scenery and abundant wildlife. Keep an eye out for deer, wild turkeys, and even the occasional black bear. Make sure to stop at the historic cabins along the way.

- **Cost:** Free, but a $5 parking tag is required.

Picnic at Cades Cove: Pack a picnic and stop at the Cades Cove Picnic Area. This is a great place for kids to run around while you enjoy lunch surrounded by the natural beauty of the Smokies.

Afternoon: Tuckaleechee Caverns

Tuckaleechee Caverns: After lunch, visit the Tuckaleechee Caverns in Townsend (about 30 minutes from Gatlinburg). These impressive underground caverns offer a cool escape from the heat and provide a fascinating look at stalactites, stalagmites, and underground waterfalls.

- **Cost:** $22 for adults, $10 for children (ages 5-11).

Evening: Dinner at Calhoun's and Ole Smoky Moonshine

Dinner at Calhoun's: Head back to Gatlinburg for a BBQ dinner at Calhoun's. Their pulled pork platter and baby back ribs are great choices for a hearty end to your day.

- **Cost:** $15-$25 per person.

Ole Smoky Moonshine (for the adults): After dinner, take a stroll to Ole Smoky Moonshine Distillery for a tasting while the kids enjoy some live music at the outdoor stage.

Day 4: Water Fun and Nature Trails

Morning: River Tubing

River Rat Tubing: Drive to nearby Townsend for a fun tubing adventure with River Rat Tubing. This lazy river float down the Little River is perfect for families, offering plenty of shallow sections and a gentle current.

- **Cost:** $20 per person, includes tube rental.

Afternoon: Nature Walk and Crafts

Elkmont Nature Walk: After tubing, head to Elkmont for a family nature walk. Elkmont is known for its historic buildings and scenic riverside paths, making it a great spot for exploration without the strenuous effort of a hike.

Arts & Crafts Community: Spend the late afternoon visiting the Great Smoky Arts & Crafts Community. Let the kids watch demonstrations, from pottery to glassblowing, and pick out a handmade souvenir.

Evening: Dinner at Crystelle Creek

Dinner at Crystelle Creek Restaurant & Grill: Enjoy dinner at Crystelle Creek, which offers a wide selection of dishes and features a lighted waterfall that the kids will love.

Cost: $15-$30 per entrée.

Day 5: Family Farewell and Scenic Drive

Morning: Roaring Fork Motor Nature Trail

Roaring Fork Motor Nature Trail: For your final day, drive the Roaring Fork Motor Nature Trail—a scenic one-way loop that features historic cabins, streams, and plenty of scenic pull-offs where you can stop and take family photos.

- **Cost:** Free, but a $5 parking tag is required.

Afternoon: Picnic and Swimming at Greenbrier

Greenbrier Picnic Area and Swimming: Pack a picnic and head to Greenbrier. The Little Pigeon River offers plenty of shallow pools where kids can wade and splash around, making it a great way to relax on your last afternoon in Gatlinburg.

Evening: Dinner and Evening Walk

Dinner at Smoky Mountain Brewery: Have a casual family dinner at the Smoky Mountain Brewery, where you can try local craft brews and enjoy classic American fare.

- **Cost:** $10-$20 per person.

Stroll Through Downtown: End your trip with a final stroll through downtown Gatlinburg, grabbing a last-minute souvenir and perhaps a funnel cake or ice cream cone from one of the many sweet shops along the Parkway.

D. Romantic Getaway: Scenic Spots and Hidden Gems

Day 1: Arrival and Sunset Views

Morning: Arrival and Check-In

Check-In at a Romantic Cabin: Start your romantic getaway by checking into a cozy cabin in the Great Smoky Arts & Crafts Community or one of the chalets overlooking the mountains. These cabins provide privacy, beautiful views, and amenities like hot tubs, fireplaces, and scenic porches that are perfect for enjoying each other's company.

Afternoon: Lunch and Scenic Ride

Lunch at Wild Plum Tea Room: Enjoy a charming lunch at the Wild Plum Tea Room, inspired by Austrian tea houses. This quaint restaurant offers a seasonal menu with dishes like lobster pie and chicken salad that are perfect for a romantic afternoon.

- **Cost:** Expect to spend $15-$25 per person.

Scenic Ride on the Aerial Tramway: After lunch, take the Aerial Tramway up to Ober Gatlinburg. The ride itself offers stunning views of the Smoky Mountains, creating the perfect setting to relax with your partner.

Evening: Sunset at Clingmans Dome

Clingmans Dome for Sunset: In the evening, drive up to Clingmans Dome—the highest point in the Smokies. The short walk up to the observation tower is rewarded with one of the most breathtaking sunset views in the region. Watching the sun dip below the horizon together is an unforgettable way to start your romantic getaway.

- **Cost:** Free, but a $5 parking tag is required.

Dinner: The Greenbrier Restaurant

Dinner at The Greenbrier: End your day with a romantic dinner at The Greenbrier, known for its sophisticated mountain lodge atmosphere and premium cuts of steak and fresh seafood. Enjoy a quiet, intimate dinner with your partner in this historic building.
Cost: $40 and up per entrée.

Day 2: Scenic Hikes and Relaxation

Morning: Romantic Hike to Grotto Falls
Hike to Grotto Falls: Start your morning with a moderate hike to Grotto Falls along the Trillium Gap Trail. This 2.6-mile round-trip hike takes you through a beautiful forest and to a waterfall you can actually walk behind, creating a perfect romantic photo opportunity.

- **Cost:** Free, but a $5 parking tag is required.

Afternoon: Spa Experience
Spa Treatment at Riverstone Resort & Spa: Treat yourselves to a couple's massage at Riverstone Resort & Spa. This luxurious experience will help you both unwind after the morning hike and set the tone for a relaxing day.

- **Cost:** $100+ per person, depending on the treatment.

Evening: Dinner and Moonshine Tasting

Dinner at Crystelle Creek Restaurant: Head to Crystelle Creek for a romantic dinner. Their garden-like outdoor seating area is beautifully lit at night and features a small creek, adding to the romantic ambiance. Try their prime rib or rainbow trout for a true taste of the Smokies.

- **Cost:** $20-$35 per entrée.

Moonshine Tasting at Sugarlands Distilling Co.: After dinner, visit Sugarlands Distilling Co. for a moonshine tasting. Sample a variety of flavors, from apple pie to butterscotch, and enjoy some live music to finish your day.

- **Cost:** $5 per tasting, includes a souvenir shot glass.

Day 3: Hidden Gems and Scenic Drives

Morning: Breakfast and Arts & Crafts Community

Breakfast at Crockett's Breakfast Camp: Start your day with a hearty Southern breakfast at Crockett's Breakfast Camp. The Black Bear Skillet or Aretha Frankenstein's Pancake Stack will provide plenty of fuel for your day of exploring.

- **Cost:** $10-$15 per person.

Explore the Great Smoky Arts & Crafts Community: Spend your morning exploring the quaint shops along the Arts & Crafts Community Loop. Find unique handmade items and chat with local artisans, all while enjoying the scenic drive through this historic area.

Afternoon: Picnic and Secret Spots

Picnic at Greenbrier Picnic Area: Pick up a picnic basket from The Cheese Cupboard in downtown Gatlinburg and head to the Greenbrier Picnic Area for a private and peaceful picnic by the Little Pigeon River. The sound of the flowing river and the surrounding woods create a naturally romantic atmosphere.

Hidden Gem at Ely's Mill: After your picnic, take a short trip to Ely's Mill—a historic site that many tourists overlook. Walk around the property, which includes the original mill, and visit the small shop with locally crafted goods.

Evening: Skylift and Stargazing

SkyLift Park and SkyBridge at Night: Ride the Gatlinburg SkyLift to SkyLift Park for a stunning view of Gatlinburg at night. Walk across the SkyBridge under the stars and enjoy the nighttime city lights from the SkyDeck.

- **Cost:** $34.95 for adults.

Late Night Dessert at The Melting Pot: End your evening with a sweet treat at The Melting Pot. Share a chocolate fondue dessert with your partner—an indulgent way to close your romantic getaway.

- **Cost:** $15-$20 per person for dessert.

Chapter 10: Gatlinburg Events and Festivals in 2025

A. Annual Festivals and Local Celebrations

Here are some of the key annual festivals and local celebrations that you won't want to miss in 2025.

1. Smoky Mountain Tunes & Tales (Summer Festival)

Smoky Mountain Tunes & Tales is a beloved summer event that turns the streets of downtown Gatlinburg into a live performance stage filled with traditional Appalachian music, storytelling, and interactive performances. Throughout the summer months, visitors can enjoy live music from local bands, watch as artisans demonstrate traditional crafts, and listen to storytellers share tales from the Smokies.

- **When:** June through early August.
- **Location:** Downtown Gatlinburg along the Parkway.
- **Highlights:** The event features musicians playing Appalachian mountain tunes, dancers performing traditional folk dances, and artisans showcasing crafts such as basket weaving and blacksmithing. This festival is perfect for families and anyone wanting to learn more about Appalachian culture.
- **Cost:** Free to attend.

2. Gatlinburg Fourth of July Midnight Parade

The Gatlinburg Fourth of July Midnight Parade is one of the most iconic events in the area, attracting thousands of visitors who come to celebrate Independence Day in style. This parade is unique because it kicks off just as the clock strikes midnight on July 4th, making it the first Independence Day parade in the nation each year. It features floats, marching bands, and performers—all decked out in red, white, and blue.

- **When:** Midnight on July 4th, 2025.
- **Location:** The parade takes place along the Parkway in downtown Gatlinburg.

- **Highlights:** Watch floats adorned with patriotic decorations, enjoy performances from local bands, and see the Gatlinburg-Pittman High School Marching Band as they lead the festivities. The unique midnight timing makes this a standout event.
- **Cost:** Free to attend.

3. Gatlinburg Chili Cookoff

The Gatlinburg Chili Cookoff is a much-anticipated annual event that takes place each fall. Featuring local chefs and restaurants competing to serve the best chili, this cookoff brings together food lovers for an evening filled with delicious flavors, live music, and a festive atmosphere. Attendees can sample a wide variety of chili, from spicy to sweet, and vote for their favorite.

- **When:** November 2025.
- **Location:** Downtown Gatlinburg.
- **Highlights:** The event includes live entertainment and music from local artists, making it a great way to kick off the holiday season in Gatlinburg. Guests can taste dozens of different chili recipes, with flavors ranging from traditional to creative, incorporating local ingredients like smoked meats and sweet corn.

- **Cost:** Admission is typically $10-$15, which includes a tasting spoon and access to all the chili samples.

4. Smoky Mountain Harvest Festival

The Smoky Mountain Harvest Festival is a citywide celebration that embraces the changing colors of fall and the warm, inviting atmosphere that comes with it. Gatlinburg is transformed with fall decorations, and many of the local businesses participate by setting up unique displays featuring pumpkins, cornstalks, and scarecrows. This festival is ideal for those who want to experience Gatlinburg at its most picturesque.

- **When:** Mid-September through November 2025.
- **Location:** Throughout Gatlinburg, with activities taking place on the Parkway and at various local attractions.
- **Highlights:** During the festival, you can visit local pumpkin patches, take part in hayrides, and enjoy seasonal treats like pumpkin pies and apple cider. The Gatlinburg SkyLift Park also hosts its own fall-themed event, complete with decorated pumpkins and scenic views.

- **Cost:** Free to attend, with some activities requiring a small fee.

5. Fantasy of Lights Christmas Parade

The Fantasy of Lights Christmas Parade is a festive highlight of Gatlinburg's holiday season, drawing crowds from across the region who come to see the spectacular floats, marching bands, and dazzling lights that fill the streets. This parade is one of the best ways to get into the holiday spirit and enjoy a winter wonderland experience in the Smokies.

- **When:** December 2025 (first Friday of the month).
- **Location:** Parkway in Downtown Gatlinburg.
- **Highlights:** The parade features over 100 entries, including elaborate floats, light displays, Santa Claus, and performances from local marching bands. The holiday decorations lining the Parkway, combined with the cheerful music and glowing lights, create a magical atmosphere.
- **Cost:** Free to attend.

6. Winter Magic Trolley Ride of Lights

The Winter Magic Trolley Ride of Lights takes place throughout the winter months, as the city lights up with millions of LED lights that transform Gatlinburg into a winter wonderland. This trolley ride offers a guided tour through downtown and along the Parkway, showcasing the holiday light displays and festive decorations.

- **When:** November 2025 to February 2026.
- **Location:** Throughout Downtown Gatlinburg and along the Parkway.
- **Highlights:** The light displays feature themes such as animals native to the Smokies, snowflakes, and traditional holiday imagery. Couples and families alike will enjoy this cozy ride, which is accompanied by holiday music and a guide providing interesting facts about the area.
- **Cost:** $5 per person for the trolley ride.

7. Hands On Gatlinburg

Hands On Gatlinburg is a unique event that allows visitors to experience the local arts and crafts culture by participating in hands-on workshops led by local artisans. During this event, you can learn how to make your own pottery, create jewelry, or craft a beautiful glass ornament. It's a wonderful way to take home a handmade souvenir and learn something new during your visit.

- **When:** April 2025 .
- **Location:** Great Smoky Arts & Crafts Community, just outside of Gatlinburg.
- **Highlights:** The workshops cater to all skill levels, and participants have the opportunity to work closely with artisans to create their own unique pieces. It's a great way to immerse yourself in the local culture and take home a one-of-a-kind keepsake.
- **Cost:** Workshop fees range from $20 to $50, depending on the type of craft and materials needed.

B. Music and Cultural Events You Can't Miss

1. Smoky Mountain Songwriters Festival

The Smoky Mountain Songwriters Festival is a celebration of the craft of songwriting, bringing together talented songwriters and musicians from across the country. Held annually in Gatlinburg, this multi-day event is packed with performances, workshops, and open mic sessions, offering visitors a behind-the-scenes look at the creative process of writing hit songs. You'll be able to hear live performances from both up-and-coming artists and well-known songwriters who have penned hits for major country and pop stars.

- **When:** August 2025 .
- **Location:** Various venues throughout downtown Gatlinburg, including outdoor stages, restaurants, and bars.
- **Highlights:** One of the unique aspects of this festival is the chance to meet and interact with songwriters, who often share the stories behind their music. The festival also hosts songwriting workshops, allowing budding musicians to learn from the best in the business.
- **Cost:** Many performances are free, though workshops and certain special events may require tickets.

2. Gatlinburg Craftsmen's Fair

The Gatlinburg Craftsmen's Fair is not just a showcase of talented artisans but also features live country, bluegrass, and gospel music that enhances the overall experience. Held twice a year, the fair features more than 200 artists and craftsmen who exhibit their handmade goods, from pottery and wood carvings to jewelry and paintings. It's a great way to immerse yourself in Appalachian culture and see the incredible craftsmanship that the Smoky Mountains are known for.

- **When:** July and October 2025.
- **Location:** Gatlinburg Convention Center.
- **Highlights:** Live music is performed daily during the fair, creating a lively and festive atmosphere. Traditional Appalachian music, bluegrass bands, and local gospel singers fill the venue with authentic sounds that pair perfectly with the handcrafted items on display.
- **Cost:** $10 admission per person, children 12 and under are free.

3. Smoky Mountain Tunes & Tales

Throughout the summer months, Gatlinburg's streets come alive with Smoky Mountain Tunes & Tales, an outdoor performance series that celebrates the rich cultural heritage of the region. The event features musicians, storytellers, dancers, and artisans dressed in traditional costumes, bringing the history and folklore of the Smokies to life. As you stroll through downtown, you'll encounter spontaneous performances, from bluegrass bands to cloggers, and even storytellers sharing tall tales of the Appalachian Mountains.

- **When:** June to August 2025.
- **Location:** Downtown Gatlinburg, along the Parkway.
- **Highlights:** The interactive nature of the event is one of its main attractions. Musicians often engage with the audience, and you'll find yourself singing along to classic tunes or learning a traditional dance. This free event is perfect for families and anyone interested in learning more about the culture and traditions of the Smoky Mountains.
- **Cost:** Free.

4. Winterfest in the Smokies

Winterfest in the Smokies is a magical time of year in Gatlinburg, where the town transforms into a winter wonderland with millions of twinkling lights, holiday displays, and festive events. The music during Winterfest adds to the enchantment, with live performances ranging from traditional holiday tunes to contemporary hits. Whether it's a concert at Ripley's Aquarium of the Smokies or a local band playing Christmas classics on the streets, there's always festive music to enjoy.

- **When:** November 2025 through February 2026.

- **Location:** Throughout downtown Gatlinburg and local venues.
- **Highlights:** The Fantasy of Lights Christmas Parade (held in early December) is one of the biggest events during Winterfest, featuring marching bands, floats, and live music. In addition, you can enjoy live performances at local restaurants and bars, where musicians play everything from jazz to bluegrass with a holiday twist.

5. Smoky Mountain Folk Festival

Held annually in nearby Lake Junaluska, just a short drive from Gatlinburg, the Smoky Mountain Folk Festival is a two-day celebration of traditional Appalachian music and dance. This event brings together some of the region's best bluegrass, old-time string bands, cloggers, and folk musicians for a series of performances that honor the heritage of the Smoky Mountains. It's an authentic cultural experience that showcases the roots of Appalachian music.

- **When:** September 2025.
- **Location:** Lake Junaluska Conference and Retreat Center (around 40 minutes from Gatlinburg).

- **Highlights:** The festival features a variety of performances, including fiddle contests, clogging demonstrations, and dulcimer music. It's a great opportunity to experience the region's traditional music in a beautiful outdoor setting.
- **Cost:** Typically $10-$20 per ticket, depending on the event.

6. Gatlinburg Songwriters' Retreat

The Gatlinburg Songwriters' Retreat is a unique cultural event that attracts both aspiring and established songwriters. This retreat offers workshops, performances, and collaboration opportunities, allowing attendees to hone their songwriting skills in the beautiful setting of the Smokies. It's not only a learning experience but also a musical showcase, with songwriters performing their original music in intimate venues.

- **When:** March 2025.
- **Location:** Various venues in Gatlinburg.
- **Highlights:** The retreat includes daily performances where participants can showcase their new songs. Workshops cover topics like lyric writing, melody composition, and music marketing.

- **Cost:** Fees vary depending on the workshop or event, with general admission for performances typically costing around $20-$40.

C. Seasonal Activities for Every Time of Year

Spring: Blossoms and Outdoor Adventures (March - May)

Spring in Gatlinburg is a magical time as the Smoky Mountains come to life with blooming wildflowers, budding trees, and fresh mountain air. This season is perfect for outdoor enthusiasts who want to explore the area's hiking trails, scenic drives, and festivals celebrating the arrival of warmer weather.

Spring Wildflower Pilgrimage: A must-do event for nature lovers, the Spring Wildflower Pilgrimage is held every April in Great Smoky Mountains National Park. This five-day event includes guided nature walks, photography tours, and educational workshops, focusing on the unique plant life of the Smokies.

- **When:** Late April 2025.
- **Cost:** Typically around $75 per person for a full event pass.
- **Location:** Various trails and sites within Great Smoky Mountains National Park.

Hiking and Scenic Drives: Spring is the ideal time to explore the park's numerous hiking trails, especially those that lead to waterfalls like Rainbow Falls or Laurel Falls. Spring rains make the waterfalls more dramatic, and the trails are alive with color from the blooming wildflowers.

Dollywood's Flower and Food Festival: While technically located in Pigeon Forge, Dollywood is just a short drive from Gatlinburg. The Flower and Food Festival offers stunning floral displays and delicious seasonal food, making it a spring highlight for families and couples alike.

- **When:** April - June 2025.
- **Cost:** $89+ for adults (Dollywood admission).

Summer: Outdoor Fun and Festivals (June - August)

Summer in Gatlinburg is packed with family-friendly activities, outdoor adventures, and vibrant festivals. The longer days allow more time to explore everything the town has to offer, from water sports to live performances in downtown.

Great Smoky Mountains National Park: Summer is the peak time for exploring the park's hiking trails, camping grounds, and picnic areas. Popular activities include tubing in the Little Pigeon River, fishing, and visiting scenic areas like Cades Cove for wildlife viewing.

Gatlinburg Fireworks Show and Midnight Parade: Celebrate Independence Day with the Gatlinburg Fourth of July Midnight Parade, followed by an impressive fireworks show over downtown Gatlinburg. It's a lively celebration filled with music, food, and plenty of fun for the whole family.

- **When:** July 3rd to 4th, 2025 (parade starts at midnight on July 4th).
- **Cost:** Free.

Rafting and Ziplining: For thrill-seekers, summer is the perfect time to go whitewater rafting on the Pigeon River or experience the adrenaline of ziplining through the Smoky Mountain canopy with companies like CLIMB Works.

- **Cost:** Rafting prices start at $45 per person, and ziplining typically costs $99+.

Fall: Stunning Foliage and Harvest Festivals (September - November)

Fall in Gatlinburg is all about the vibrant colors of changing leaves, cool mountain air, and the cozy feeling of the harvest season. This is the best time to take in the breathtaking views of the Smokies' famous fall foliage while also enjoying local festivals and seasonal flavors.

Smoky Mountain Harvest Festival: From mid-September through November, Gatlinburg transforms for the Smoky Mountain Harvest Festival, with pumpkin displays, fall decor, and special events throughout the town. Visitors can enjoy hayrides, visit local pumpkin patches, and taste seasonal treats like pumpkin pie and apple cider.

- **When:** September - November 2025.
- **Cost:** Free.

Oktoberfest at Ober Gatlinburg: Held annually at Ober Gatlinburg, this German-themed festival brings Bavarian culture to the Smokies with traditional music, dancing, and food. You can enjoy bratwurst, pretzels, and German beer while watching performances from authentic oompah bands.

- **When:** October 2025.
- **Cost:** Free admission, with additional costs for food and drinks.

Autumn Colors and Scenic Drives: Fall is the perfect season for taking scenic drives along

Newfound Gap Road or the Blue Ridge Parkway. The vibrant hues of red, orange, and yellow foliage make for unforgettable photo opportunities. Clingmans Dome is another must-visit for panoramic fall views from the highest point in the Smokies.

Winter: Snowy Fun and Holiday Magic (December - February)

Winter in Gatlinburg turns the town into a winter wonderland, with festive lights, snowy mountain peaks, and plenty of holiday events. Whether you're into skiing, cozying up by the fire, or enjoying the local holiday parades, winter in Gatlinburg has something for everyone.

Winterfest and Trolley Ride of Lights: From late November through February, Gatlinburg is illuminated with millions of twinkling lights during Winterfest. Hop on the Trolley Ride of Lights to see the stunning holiday displays along the Parkway.

- **When:** November 2025 - February 2026.
- **Cost:** $5 per person for the trolley ride.

Skiing and Snowboarding at Ober Gatlinburg: Winter is ski season in Gatlinburg, and Ober Gatlinburg offers both skiing and snowboarding on a variety of slopes. Even if you're not into skiing, you can enjoy snow tubing, ice skating, or simply taking in the mountain views from the Aerial Tramway.

- **Cost:** Lift tickets start at $45 for adults, with equipment rentals available.

Fantasy of Lights Christmas Parade: Held every December, the Fantasy of Lights Christmas Parade features floats, marching bands, and, of course, Santa Claus. This parade is one of Gatlinburg's biggest holiday events and a must-see if you're visiting during the Christmas season.

- **When:** Early December 2025 (first Friday).
- **Cost:** Free.

Chapter 11: Practical Travel Tips

A. Weather and What to Pack

Spring (March - May)

Weather: Spring in Gatlinburg is beautiful, with blooming wildflowers and fresh mountain air, but temperatures can be unpredictable. Early spring (March) tends to be cool, with temperatures ranging between 40°F and 60°F (4°C to 15°C), while late spring (May) can be much warmer, with temperatures rising to 70°F to 80°F (21°C to 27°C). Rain is common, so be prepared for occasional showers.

What to Pack:

- **Light Jacket and Rain Gear:** Bring a light waterproof jacket or windbreaker, as well as an umbrella or a compact rain poncho for unexpected showers.

- **Layers:** Spring mornings and evenings can be chilly, so pack layers that you can easily remove, such as long-sleeve shirts, sweaters, and lightweight pullovers.

Comfortable Shoes: Trails can be muddy, so waterproof hiking boots or sturdy walking shoes are a must if you plan on exploring the national park.

Summer (June - August)

Weather: Summer in Gatlinburg is warm and often humid, with temperatures ranging from 65°F to 85°F (18°C to 29°C). It's also the wettest time of the year, with occasional afternoon thunderstorms.

What to Pack:

- **Lightweight Clothing:** Opt for breathable fabrics like cotton or moisture-wicking activewear to keep you comfortable in the humidity. Shorts, tank tops, and T-shirts are perfect for exploring during the day.
- **Swimsuit:** Pack a swimsuit for tubing in the rivers or visiting Ober Gatlinburg's water attractions.
- **Sunscreen and Hat:** The sun can be strong, especially if you're hiking or spending time

outdoors. Pack sunscreen, a wide-brimmed hat, and sunglasses to protect yourself.

Fall (September - November)

Weather: Fall is one of the most popular times to visit Gatlinburg, thanks to the stunning foliage. Temperatures range from 45°F to 70°F (7°C to 21°C), with cooler evenings as the season progresses.

What to Pack:

- **Warm Layers:** During fall, layers are your best friend. Pack sweaters, flannel shirts, and light to mid-weight jackets for chilly mornings and evenings.
- **Comfortable Footwear:** Hiking boots are ideal for exploring the colorful trails in the Smokies. A good pair of wool socks will also help keep your feet warm on cooler days.
- **Scarf and Gloves:** As the temperatures drop in late fall, scarves, gloves, and a hat may come in handy, particularly for early morning or late evening activities.

Winter (December - February)

Weather: Winter in Gatlinburg is typically cold, with temperatures ranging from 25°F to 50°F (-4°C to 10°C). Snow is possible, particularly at higher elevations, making it a great time for skiing or tubing at Ober Gatlinburg.

What to Pack:

- **Heavy Jacket:** A heavy winter coat or insulated jacket is essential for keeping warm during your winter adventures.
- **Cold Weather Accessories:** Bring gloves, a knit hat, and a scarf to stay warm. If you plan on visiting higher elevations, snow gear like thermal underwear can also be helpful.
- **Waterproof Boots:** If you're visiting for winter activities like skiing or snow tubing, pack waterproof boots to keep your feet dry in the snow.

Additional Packing Tips for All Seasons

- **Daypack:** Carry a small backpack for day trips, especially if you plan on hiking or exploring the Smokies. Include essentials like water, snacks, a first-aid kit, and a rain poncho.
- **Reusable Water Bottle:** Staying hydrated is crucial, especially in the summer months or while hiking. A reusable water bottle is a

must-have, and many trails have spots where you can refill it.

- **Bug Spray:** In the warmer months, insect repellent will help keep mosquitoes and other pests away while you enjoy outdoor activities.
- **Binoculars and Camera:** The Smoky Mountains are teeming with wildlife and scenic vistas. Bringing binoculars and a good camera can enhance your experience and help capture those special moments.

B. Travel Safety and Emergency Contacts

General Safety Tips

1. Stay on Marked Trails: The Great Smoky Mountains National Park offers beautiful hikes, but it's important to always stay on designated trails. Wandering off the paths can be dangerous, as it may lead to disorientation or put you at risk of encountering wildlife. Before setting out, inform someone of your plans and expected return time.

2. Be Bear Aware: Gatlinburg is surrounded by the Smoky Mountains, which are home to black bears. To minimize the risk of bear encounters, keep all food stored securely and use bear-proof containers where possible. If you see a bear, keep your distance—at least 50 yards—and do not approach it for photos.

3. Weather Awareness: Gatlinburg's weather, especially in the mountains, can change rapidly. Check the weather forecast each day before heading out. In case of thunderstorms or heavy rain, it's best to stay off the trails and avoid river crossings.

4. Stay Hydrated: The Smokies are beautiful, but hiking can be strenuous, particularly in the heat of summer. Always carry enough water for your hike and stay hydrated throughout the day. Dehydration is a common issue for hikers who underestimate the difficulty of some trails.

5. Avoid Driving Under the Influence: Gatlinburg has several popular wineries and distilleries. If you plan on sampling local moonshine or wine, consider using a taxi, rideshare service, or the Gatlinburg Trolley to avoid driving after drinking.

6. Know Your Limitations: The elevation changes in the Smokies can make some trails more challenging than they appear. Choose hikes that match your fitness level and avoid pushing yourself beyond your comfort zone. If you're traveling with children or elderly family members, opt for shorter trails that are more accessible.

Emergency Contacts

When traveling, it's always a good idea to have key emergency contacts and addresses written down or saved on your phone. Below is a list of useful numbers and services to keep in mind during your stay in Gatlinburg.

1. Gatlinburg Police Department

- **Emergency:** Dial 911 for immediate assistance in emergencies requiring police, fire, or medical help.
- **Non-Emergency Contact:** (865) 436-5181. For non-urgent issues, the Gatlinburg Police Department is available for assistance. Their services include lost property reports, general inquiries, and local law enforcement matters.

2. Gatlinburg Fire Department

- **Emergency:** Dial 911.
- **Non-Emergency Contact:** (865) 436-5112. The Gatlinburg Fire Department provides services for fire emergencies, rescue operations, and safety information. Gatlinburg's mountainous terrain means the risk of wildfires can be higher, especially

during dry spells, so always heed fire safety guidelines.

3. Great Smoky Mountains National Park Dispatch

- **Emergency Contact:** Dial 911 for any emergencies within the park, such as injuries, lost hikers, or other urgent situations.
- **Visitor Information:** (865) 436-1200. This number can connect you to park rangers for non-emergency situations such as trail conditions, road closures, or wildlife sightings.

4. Local Medical Services

LeConte Medical Center: The LeConte Medical Center in nearby Sevierville provides full medical services in case of illness or injury.

- **Address:** 742 Middle Creek Rd, Sevierville, TN 37862.
- **Phone:** (865) 446-7000.

Urgent Care Facilities: There are also several urgent care centers in the area, including AFC Urgent Care Sevierville at (865) 429-9110, which can provide quick medical assistance for non-life-threatening issues.

5. Poison Control

- **Tennessee Poison Center:** Dial 1-800-222-1222 for poison-related emergencies. If you or someone in your party comes into contact with a poisonous plant, insect, or ingests something harmful, this hotline provides immediate assistance and advice.

6. Roadside Assistance

AAA Roadside Assistance: If you're a AAA member, you can contact their roadside assistance for vehicle issues, such as a breakdown or flat tire.

- **Phone:** 1-800-AAA-HELP (1-800-222-4357).

Local Towing Services: Gatlinburg Towing & Recovery is available to assist if you encounter car troubles.

- **Phone:** (865) 436-9584.

7. Gatlinburg Welcome Center

The Gatlinburg Welcome Center is a great resource for tourists. They offer maps, brochures, and advice to make your trip enjoyable.

- **Address:** 1011 Banner Rd, Gatlinburg, TN 37738.
- **Phone:** (865) 430-4148.
- **Hours:** Typically open 8:30 a.m. to 5:00 p.m. daily.

Safety Tips for Wildlife Encounters

Gatlinburg is located in the heart of the Smokies, meaning encounters with wildlife are not uncommon. Here are some additional safety tips:

- **Do Not Feed Wildlife:** Feeding animals can make them dependent on humans and more aggressive. It's also illegal in the park to feed or disturb wildlife.
- **Keep Your Distance:** Always stay at least 50 yards away from bears and 25 yards from other wildlife, such as deer and elk.
- **Bear Spray:** Carrying bear spray is recommended if you plan to hike in areas known for bear activity. Bear spray can be effective in deterring an aggressive bear but should only be used as a last resort.

C. Essential Apps for Exploring Gatlinburg

1. AllTrails

AllTrails is an excellent app for those planning to explore the extensive trail network within the Great Smoky Mountains National Park It offers detailed information on hundreds of trails, including difficulty ratings, elevation profiles, trail maps, and reviews from other hikers. Whether you're an experienced hiker or a beginner, AllTrails can help you choose the perfect route based on your preferences.

- **Features:** Offline maps, GPS tracking, and downloadable trail information, so you can navigate even when you're out of cell range.
- **Why You Need It:** Gatlinburg's proximity to the Smokies means there are a lot of trail options, and this app ensures you can find a suitable one with ease and confidence.
- **Cost:** The app is free, but a premium version is available for $29.99/year, offering additional features like offline navigation.

2. Gatlinburg Tours

Gatlinburg Tours is a must-have app that provides self-guided audio tours of Gatlinburg's most iconic attractions and hidden gems. The app offers interesting historical insights, cultural anecdotes, and helpful recommendations as you stroll through town, letting you explore at your own pace without missing important highlights.

- **Features:** Audio guide tours, offline maps, and itineraries tailored to your interests (history, nature, food, etc.).

- **Why You Need It:** Whether you're visiting popular spots like the SkyLift Park or exploring downtown Gatlinburg, the app provides a handy guide without the cost of hiring a personal tour guide.
- **Cost:** Free to download; specific audio tours cost $5-$10 each.

3. Smoky Mountains Visitor Guide

The Smoky Mountains Visitor Guide app provides up-to-date information on Great Smoky Mountains National Park, including trail maps, visitor center locations, and current weather conditions. It also lists upcoming events, special programs, and closures within the park, making it easy to plan your trip.

- **Features:** Maps of the national park, safety alerts, event listings, and park rules.
- **Why You Need It:** This app is ideal for staying informed about trail conditions and park events, helping you to make the most out of your time in the Smokies.
- **Cost:** Free.

4. Uber/Lyft

Although Gatlinburg is a walkable town, Uber and Lyft are excellent options for those times when you need a ride, especially when visiting attractions located on the outskirts of town or after sampling some local moonshine. Both apps provide reliable and convenient transportation services for getting around town, particularly in the evenings when public transport options are limited.

- **Why You Need It:** The Gatlinburg Trolley is great, but it doesn't operate late into the night, making rideshare apps convenient after dinner or a late-night show.
- **Cost:** Free to download; cost per ride depends on the distance.

5. Great Smoky Mountains Weather App

Having access to accurate, up-to-date weather information is crucial, especially when planning hikes in the Great Smoky Mountains. The Great Smoky Mountains Weather App provides real-time weather alerts, detailed forecasts, and notifications about changing conditions, so you're never caught off-guard by a sudden storm.

- **Features:** Hourly forecasts, radar imagery, and severe weather alerts for Gatlinburg and surrounding areas.

- **Why You Need It:** Mountain weather can be unpredictable, and this app helps you stay informed and make safe decisions when hiking or exploring the area.
- **Cost:** Free, with in-app purchases for premium features.

6. Gatlinburg Trolley Tracker

The Gatlinburg Trolley Tracker app provides real-time information on the Gatlinburg Trolley system, making it easier to navigate the town and reach popular destinations without worrying about parking. The app allows you to see trolley routes, schedules, and arrival times, ensuring you can plan your day efficiently.

- **Features:** Real-time tracking, estimated arrival times, route maps, and schedules.
- **Why You Need It:** Gatlinburg's streets can get crowded, and finding parking can be a hassle during peak seasons. The trolley is an economical and environmentally friendly way to explore.
- **Cost:** Free.

7. OpenTable

OpenTable is the perfect app for making reservations at some of Gatlinburg's best restaurants. With the popularity of spots like The Peddler Steakhouse and Cherokee Grill, using OpenTable can ensure you secure a table without a long wait, especially during busy weekends or the peak tourist season.

- **Features:** View menus, read reviews, and book reservations in real-time.
- **Why You Need It:** Many of Gatlinburg's popular restaurants can have long waits, especially during busy seasons. Using OpenTable helps you plan ahead and enjoy stress-free dining.
- **Cost:** Free.

8. Google Maps and Google Translate

Google Maps is essential for getting around Gatlinburg, whether you're walking downtown, driving to Cades Cove, or exploring the more remote parts of the national park. Google Translate may also come in handy if you encounter any language barriers, particularly when interacting with international visitors or trying to read informational signs written in multiple languages.

- **Features:** GPS navigation, local business reviews, and offline maps (for areas with no cell service).
- **Why You Need It:** Navigation in the mountains can be challenging, and Google Maps provides reliable directions, even on the smaller, winding roads leading to some of Gatlinburg's hidden gems.
- **Cost:** Free.

9. TripAdvisor

TripAdvisor is an excellent tool for checking reviews, recommendations, and ratings of Gatlinburg's attractions, restaurants, and hotels. It's especially helpful for getting real insights from other travelers and ensuring you're making informed choices when deciding what to do or where to eat.

- **Features:** Traveler reviews, photo galleries, Q&A sections, and booking options.
- **Why You Need It:** Planning your visit can be easier when you can rely on the experiences of others. TripAdvisor offers comprehensive information to help you prioritize what's worth seeing.
- **Cost:** Free.

10. First Aid by American Red Cross

Accidents can happen, especially when exploring nature. The First Aid by American Red Cross app provides quick, easy-to-follow instructions for handling minor injuries like cuts, burns, and insect bites. Having this app on your phone can provide peace of mind, particularly when venturing into remote areas of the Smoky Mountains.

- **Features:** Step-by-step first-aid guidance, emergency information, and preloaded content for offline access.
- **Why You Need It:** Whether you're hiking, camping, or exploring the area, this app can provide crucial first-aid information when needed, even without internet access.
- **Cost:** Free.

Conclusion

Welcome to Gatlinburg Travel Guide 2025! We are thrilled that you've chosen this book to help navigate the charm and beauty of Gatlinburg and the Smoky Mountains. It's been our pleasure to bring you closer to one of the most captivating regions in the Appalachian range, and we sincerely hope that this guide has enhanced your journey—whether it's your first visit or a return trip to this picturesque mountain town.

In this guide, we've worked to provide you with a well-rounded overview of Gatlinburg, highlighting its stunning natural landscapes, historic charm, and vibrant culture. From the bustling streets of downtown to the tranquil trails in Great Smoky Mountains National Park, we've covered essential information such as travel tips, accommodation options, dining experiences, and the best ways to get around—ensuring that your visit is as seamless and enjoyable as possible.

We hope the descriptions of popular attractions like Gatlinburg SkyLift Park, the Ripley's Aquarium of the Smokies, and the scenic vistas of Clingmans Dome have inspired you to explore everything Gatlinburg has to offer. Whether you're seeking adventure through hiking, ziplining, or skiing, or just looking to relax and enjoy a romantic getaway in a mountain cabin, Gatlinburg has something for everyone. Our sections on local culture and artisan crafts also introduced you to the town's rich Appalachian heritage, showcasing the traditions and creativity that make Gatlinburg a unique and welcoming destination.

For history lovers, we've shared stories about Gatlinburg's early settlers, the role of the Smokies in local folklore, and how this region has evolved into the charming town it is today. Understanding this history can make your visit even more meaningful as you walk the same paths once traveled by the region's first pioneers.

We've also provided practical travel advice, including what to pack, safety guidelines, and the best times to visit each attraction. From family-friendly adventures to the area's most romantic spots, we've tailored this guide to meet the diverse needs of all travelers. We hope our recommendations on local festivals, outdoor adventures, and culinary delights have added to the magic of your visit and helped you experience the very best of the Smokies.

As your time in Gatlinburg comes to an end, we encourage you to reflect on the experiences you've had, from the breathtaking mountain views to the warm hospitality of the local community. Gatlinburg isn't just a destination—it's a place where you can make lasting memories, connect with nature, and embrace the spirit of adventure. We hope that the sights, sounds, and flavors of the Smoky Mountains will stay with you long after your trip ends.

Thank you for choosing Gatlinburg Travel Guide 2025 to accompany you on your journey. We hope it's been a helpful and inspiring companion, guiding you through every step of your Smoky Mountain adventure. May your travels continue to be full of wonder and joy, and may Gatlinburg always hold a special place in your heart.

Until we meet again, happy trails, and may the mountains always call you back.

Safe travels and all the best!

Warm regards,
The Gatlinburg Travel Guide 2025 Team

A Note to Our Valued Readers

Dear Traveler,

We want to extend our heartfelt gratitude for choosing the "**Gatlinburg Travel Guide 2025**" as your companion for exploring this beautiful destination. We hope it has enhanced your experience and brought the Smoky Mountains to life during your adventure.

We would be incredibly grateful if you could take a moment to share your thoughts by leaving a review. Your honest feedback not only helps other travelers discover and make the most of this guide but also encourages us to keep improving and bringing you even better content in the future.

Thank you for being a part of our journey, and we look forward to accompanying you on many more adventures.

Warm regards,
Albert N. Allred

Exclusive Bonus: Smoky Mountain Recipes

As a special bonus for choosing the "Gatlinburg Travel Guide 2025," we've included a selection of traditional Smoky Mountain recipes and preparation instructions to help you enjoy a taste of Appalachian cuisine at home. These recipes feature classic Southern flavors that will make you feel like you're right in the heart of the Smokies.

1. Tennessee Cornbread

Ingredients:

- 1 cup yellow cornmeal
- 1 cup flour
- 1 tablespoon sugar
- 1 teaspoon salt
- 1 teaspoon baking powder
- 1/2 teaspoon baking soda
- 1 cup buttermilk
- 2 large eggs
- 1/4 cup melted butter

Instructions:

1. Preheat oven to 400°F (200°C) and grease a cast-iron skillet.
2. In a bowl, mix the cornmeal, flour, sugar, salt, baking powder, and baking soda
3. In a separate bowl, whisk together the buttermilk, eggs, and melted butter.

4. Combine the wet ingredients with the dry ingredients and mix until smooth.
5. Pour the batter into the skillet and bake for 20-25 minutes, or until golden brown.

2. Smoky Mountain Trout Almondine

Ingredients:

- 2 fresh trout fillets
- 1/4 cup flour
- Salt and pepper to taste
- 1/4 cup slivered almonds
- 4 tablespoons butter
- Juice of 1 lemon
- 1 tablespoon chopped parsley

Instructions:

1. Season the trout fillets with salt and pepper and dust with flour.
2. In a skillet over medium heat, melt 2 tablespoons of butter and cook the trout for 3-4 minutes per side until golden brown. Remove from the skillet.
3. In the same skillet, melt the remaining butter, add the almonds, and cook until lightly toasted.
4. Add the lemon juice and pour the almond-butter sauce over the trout.
5. Garnish with chopped parsley and serve hot.

3. Appalachian Apple Stack Cake

Ingredients:

- 2 cups flour
- 1 teaspoon baking powder
- 1/2 teaspoon baking soda
- 1 teaspoon ground cinnamon
- 1/2 teaspoon ground ginger
- 1 cup buttermilk
- 1/2 cup molasses
- 1/2 cup sugar
- 1 egg
- 4 cups dried apples
- 1 cup water
- 1/2 cup brown sugar

Instructions:

1. Preheat oven to 350°F (175°C). Grease and flour 2 round cake pans.
2. Mix the flour, baking powder, baking soda, cinnamon, and ginger in a bowl.
3. In a separate bowl, combine the buttermilk, molasses, sugar, and egg. Add to the flour mixture and stir until smooth.
4. Divide the batter between the cake pans and bake for 20-25 minutes.
5. In a saucepan, cook the dried apples with water and brown sugar until the apples are soft.
6. Stack the cake layers, spreading the apple mixture between each layer.

4. Smoky Mountain BBQ Pulled Pork

Ingredients:

- 3 lbs pork shoulder
- 1 tablespoon paprika
- 1 tablespoon brown sugar
- 1 teaspoon garlic powder
- 1 teaspoon onion powder
- 1 teaspoon salt
- 1 teaspoon black pepper
- 1 cup BBQ sauce
- 1/2 cup apple cider vinegar

Instructions:

1. Mix the paprika, brown sugar, garlic powder, onion powder, salt, and pepper together and rub all over the pork shoulder.
2. Place the pork in a slow cooker and add the apple cider vinegar. Cook on low for 8 hours.
3. Once the pork is tender, shred with two forks and mix with BBQ sauce.
4. Serve on buns with coleslaw.

5. Blackberry Cobbler

Ingredients:

- 2 cups fresh blackberries
- 1 cup sugar

- 1 cup flour
- 1 teaspoon baking powder
- 1/4 teaspoon salt
- 1 cup milk
- 1/2 cup melted butter

Instructions:

1. Preheat oven to 375°F (190°C).
2. In a mixing bowl, combine the flour, baking powder, salt, and sugar.
3. Stir in the milk until the batter is smooth, then pour in the melted butter.
4. Spread the blackberries evenly in a greased baking dish and pour the batter over them.
5. Bake for 35-40 minutes, or until the top is golden and crispy.

Made in the USA
Las Vegas, NV
17 January 2025